How to Butcher Livestock and Game

By
Paul Peacock

Published by The Good Life Press Ltd 2007

ISBN 978 1 9048 7128 6

A catalogue record for this book is available from
the British Library.

Published by
The Good Life Press Ltd
PO Box 536
Preston
PR2 9ZY
www.farmingbooksandvideos.com
www.thegoodlifepress.co.uk

Cover design by Firecatcher Books
Drawings by Rebecca Peacock and Josh Peacock
Set by The Good Life Press Ltd.
Printed and bound in Great Britain by Cromwell Press.

How to Butcher Livestock and Game

By
Paul Peacock

Contents

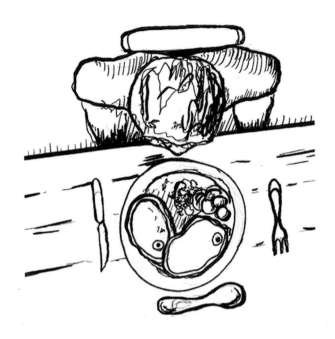

Introduction

Slaughter begins at birth

I have chosen to subtitle the introduction to this book for a very good reason. As far as I am concerned this is the most important part of the book and deals with why we rear animals to be killed and eaten.

When you get down to it an animal kept for meat is destined to be killed and eaten. You might think this to be a horrid, inhumane and even careless statement but that is not so! If an animal is going to die for my dinner, for the health and development of my family, my land and my home, I owe it a debt I cannot really repay. It has a special rank; an honoured position that befits its status. While it is alive the least it deserves is the very best care I can provide. In addition its death must be swift and painless and unknown to the animal. Its treatment when it becomes food must also be respectful and complete.

In essence this book is about a compromise. In one respect it is about a complete lack of compromise which is required when it comes to animal welfare and this prerequisite is fundamental to this book. Then, beneath this, are a series of compromises that have to be addressed.

The first of these compromises is the realisation that we have to be sure in our own minds about the killing of an animal for food. The line separating feeling like a murderer for killing a chicken and enjoying a Sunday roast is perhaps all too narrow. Even John Seymour, the so called modern father of self-sufficiency who killed all of his own meat when he had a farm, had this same dilemma to an extent. He worried about how long his animals lived and thought that six months was far too short a life for a pig, so he killed them at a greater age, often at over eighteen months. By that time they had usually become huge, fatty and often tainted, but this was something he felt comfortable with.

There are those who, with an air of machismo, will tell of their prowess in dispatching animals as though everyone should be able to do it without any hint of squeamishness or remorse. You will not find this book so callous. The decision to kill something in order to eat it should never, in my opinion at least, be lightly taken.

We must also accept that the only viable way of killing any animal is to use violence. They also don't always take the transport from farm animal to food so easily. Their cries complain vigorously about the experience and they inevitably die with their eyes open; the pathway to death cannot always be guaranteed to be simple, painless and in line with our human sensibilities.

The first compromise is threfore an internal one; can I kill an animal and still then be able to eat it?

I saw a video of how one village killed its pigs somewhere in Eastern Europe. They brought the animal into the street, happy as anything. Then the man took out a sharp knife and slit its throat. Of course, the pig went mad! It thrashed around, screamed and gurgled in its own blood and then finally fell over and died. They set it on fire to remove the hairs and the women of the village fought over its ears that had been cooked in the process. They all thought it was great fun! I am pretty certain the pig did not.

Although it may be different for you, the compromise for me about eating animals is two fold. Can I kill the animal without causing it pain, or at least as little as possible, and can I treat it with complete dignity. Whichever way you look at it the animal has given its life for my sustenance, and consequently it should quite rightly deserve a great deal of respect from me. So important is this to me that if I cannot fulfil these criteria I really cannot eat meat at all.

John Seymour said that unless you were prepared to kill an animal yourself you shouldn't really keep animals for meat. Well for me the whole thing is a little more complex. Not everyone can rear and kill meat. Most people have to rely on shops as their provider. These people can, however, insist on buying meat that has come from a source that has the very highest standards of animal care. And this leads us to yet another another implication.

You can buy a chicken breast from the supermarket for a third of the price you might pay at a butchers who do their own killing, although such places are now few and far between. The price of cheap meat certainly undercuts the best butchers and, in the end, we all lose out because there will be no real butchers left.

This cheaper meat is, however, paid for in another way. The costs that are cut in getting tonnes and tonnes of inexpensive chicken breasts into the supermarkets is paid for by the chickens themselves through the corners which are inevitably cut in their welfare to achieve this absurdly low price. Broiler chickens, the kind you buy in supermarkets for a couple of pounds, live their lives in truly squalid condition as we shall see later. My hens and your hens can actually live like chicken royalty free from the nightmare of being swept about in a huge dark shed by tens of thousands of frightened birds. Indeed, even their deaths can be quick and easy.

For a start, my birds are happier, and, having written that, I can hear the chuckles of intensive farmers everywhere. But I feel better eating my own birds in the knowledge that the lives they have led are so much better than those of their battery housed compatriots who have been kept in the dark, overheated and overfed to satisfy a cheap food culture. The financial cost to me for my table bird is probably more than the cost of buying a supermarket chicken but the bird has paid with its life and that is enough. At least it hasn't also paid the price of 90 days of unnatural discomfort.

To my mind I have a contract with my animals. I care for them, keep them in humane conditions, feed them, treat them with respectful care and, when I kill them, I do the job as proficiently and painlessly as possible. And then, when the killing is over, the whole animal is used without waste. If I cannot use the entire animal I don't kill it. It might sound silly but why should it die and some of it simply be thrown away for the sake of convenience?

There are many reasons why people choose, quite rightly, not to kill their animals. Perhaps they do not have the right facilities to kill and eviscerate an animal as large as a pig. Maybe they live close to people who would be horrified at the thought of the nice chickens wandering around the garden ending up on your plate. Nobody wants the RSPCA turning up every time you have a Sunday roast!

There is nothing wrong with sending your animals to the local abattoir for slaughter and receiving their carcass ready for you to butcher yourself or even already prepared. This book is about producing your own food, whether you have killed it yourself or got someone else to do it for you.

There is much to be said about the home farmer leading the way, not only for animal welfare but in the way we process and cook our meat too. In the UK we have done away with many of our local abattoirs, and a huge number of butchers have gone to the wall because the majority of people buy their meat from supermarkets. But the time is coming when we are going to need our local butchers back. Imagine taking a dozen chickens into the supermarket for the butcher to kill; he'd run a mile!

So this book has two themes running throughout its length, both intertwined. Animal welfare and professionalism and an aspiration to achieve the very best in both fields.

While researching this book I asked a lot of people how they killed their animals. Some of the responses came from New Zealand, America, Europe, and even Africa, as well as the UK. The overriding impression that came from the research was a sorry mix of the comedic and the dangerously illegal. Quite frankly the lengths that people will got to in order to remove the perceived squeamishness from killing their stock is frightening.

On the whole people kill chickens more than any other stock animal. This is simply because there are more people keeping chickens than anything else. Rabbits and pigeons are usually shot in the wild. And though there is at least one company that collects rabbits from individuals for slaughter and processing, it is quite unusual for people to kill captive rabbits solely for domestic use.

I found examples of people putting chickens in containers of petrol or ether in order to kill them , blowing their heads off with a .410 bore shotgun and even hiding behind the hen house and ambushing the poor animal with a frying pan. A large number of people use firearms but there was a general lack of understanding about which weapon was best for which beast.

There was a lot of confusion about what is lawful in terms of killing livestock, particularly chickens. Literature from around the world is often unhelpful because the treatments, methods and equipment are not the same. Custom and practice account for a large part of the laws pertaining to animal slaughter around the world. In some countries you can legally kill an animal without stunning it, but in the UK this is only the case in certain tightly controlled circumstances.

When it came to captive bolt stunning many people were confused about the role of the tool in stunning and were surprised to hear that in many cases the equipment would not kill the animal. People contemplating the future killing of animals talked a lot about the use of a humane killer as though it was some type of pain free, mess free and sterile means of dispatch. It came as a shock that for most cases the mode of death in slaughter was the irrevocable loss of blood. Moreover, a large number of people did not realise, because they hadn't done it, that the captive bolt gun has to actually touch the head in a certain place, and that they would have to stick a knife into its neck and cause the animal to bleed.

There was also confusion about the position on the skull required to effectively stun a large animal and the suffering caused by inappropriate use of equipment. Where you placed the captive bolt stunner on a sheep and a cow are quite different and this was not always evident in people's responses.

There was certainly a lot of misunderstanding about the use of free bullets. I blame John Seymour for this because he wrote in many of his books about enticing the animal into the barn and shooting it in the head with a .22 bullet. Goodness knows how many people have done this with no thought of the amount of energy invested in a piece of lead that is travelling faster than a jet plane, and that it is very likely to exit the skull and leave you with a lot more than a dead pig on your hands.

One of the cornerstones of this book is that people should be able, if they want, to kill their own animals for their own food. It would be far easier to become a vegetarian and cop out of the responsibility of all this killing stuff. But in essence, this is what self-reliance is all about; accepting responsibility. Perhaps you could say that vegans should not travel in vehicles of any kind, live in houses, walk the streets, wear most clothes, wash with detergents of any kind or take medicines. It is all too easy to say 'I am a vegetarian and I do not cause any animal to suffer.' Some of the animal rights people certainly do have a point, though, especially if some of the responses to my small and possibly unscientific, survey are in any way accurate.

Killing animals at home should be the pinnacle of animal welfare. If we cannot provide this then in all conscience an animal is better killed by an experienced slaughter-man. By killing an animal at home we are avoiding a journey in traffic, a journey often far longer than it needs be to thanks to successive governments promoting a society where abattoirs are rapidly reducing in number. We also prevent the animal from smelling the blood and experiencing a frightening and alien world that leads to their death via a conveyor belt and the noise of the unusual (to the animal at least) contraptions for restraining the beast prior to stunning.

We should regard death at home as the very best

way of doing the job and prove this to be better than the 'professionals.' All other forms of killing and butchering must, by necessitating transport and the requirement to kill lots of animals at the same time, be less desirable than any home killing. The responses to my little survey suggest that we have a long way to go.

When I talked to people while preparing this book I had a pang of guilt. Chanticlear was the first animal I ever killed. He was a cockerel and, to be honest, I didn't plan to kill him for food. I planned to kill him because he got on my nerves! He was one of those French (not that I have anything against the French – save the rugby players!) birds that they used to throw on the pitch at international rugby matches, and he was so bossy that all the ladies of his harem were not even allowed to eat or drink without him ripping bits out of them. What follows is a bit of history….

I inherited Chanticlear. He was on an allotment where birds were kept by the plot holders, which was quite unusual in my town. The man who had the plot before me simply ignored his birds and I found rotting carcasses and skeletons all over the place. He just sat there and watched them die. I think Chanticlear may have been a fighting cock, though I never knew.

The previous owner was evicted from the allotment and I was allowed to take over the plot and set about cleaning it up. A lady who lived on a housing estate had been told by the council to get rid of her birds because someone complained of rats, and so I ended up with a set of six beautiful Rhode Island Reds on the proviso that her young daughter could come and see them.

She did come, but Chanticlear had ripped one of them to bits and the poor child went home went home in tears. Enough was enough so the pot beckoned. I picked him up on half a dozen occasions and he nearly killed me each time. I was angry and I knew I had to remove the huge menacing presence that was Chanticlear. He was a hateful being and it made me angry just to look at him. As I finally held him in my shed I saw, in the corner of my eye, the hens running for the food hopper, glad he was not around to cause them harm. I hated him and felt that and he deserved what was coming.

For that reason very reason I could not bring myself to do the job. The thought of killing this animal in anger was just not right and was somehow beneath me. From that day I made a rule; while it's alive it has a right to be itself. Once it's dead, it's food, but both of these states require their own unique care, planning and love.

Eventually Chanticlear did end up in the pot but only after a considerable time spent in solitary confinement but that's another story!

Paul Peacock
Manchester 2007

How to Butcher Livestock and Game

Chapter One
Do you really really want to do this?

Before we look at killing animals in the later chapters, we need to be sure of many things. So far as British law goes, and very many countries around the world follow suit in a similar manner, we incorporated EU law in 1993 that states that no one can slaughter an animal without holding the required slaughter licence unless the animal:

- Is being killed for the purposes of disease control.
- Is being killed by means of a free bullet in the field (in such instances, the individual should hold the relevant firearms certificate)
- Is suffering and is being killed for emergency reasons relating to the welfare of the animal and where the animal needs to be killed/slaughtered immediately.
- Is being killed by its owner for his private consumption.
- Is being killed by a qualified veterinary surgeon.

Notice that the proviso *'is being killed by its owner for his private consumption'* is singular and strongly infers that this food cannot legally be given to family members, friends and must certainly not be sold.

In both England and Wales the interpretation errs on the side of not giving meat to family members, though there is some debate about whether the family is a part of the combined ownership of the animal. In more remote areas it is thought that the need to be able to slaughter a pig or a sheep or even a cow at home is more important because of the likely remoteness of the smallholder. It would therefore be unfair to expect a man to eat his own cow and have to drive 40 miles to buy meat for his family.

However, there are moves to outlaw completely the home killing of animals for food, firstly because of disease control, secondly for financial considerations and thirdly for reasons of animal welfare. A number of scientific reports have stated that, in their opinion, the home killing of animals, even for personal consumption, is dangerous and must be stopped because it is difficult to ensure that certain organisms do not enter the human food chain. These moves, indeed all the laws pertaining to the slaughter of animals, show how far we have come from the peasant society we once were. The need to ensure the balance between animal welfare and a controlled and disease free supply of meat for the population forces us to buy from the supermarket.

Fortunately there is still provision for the home slaughter of animals, mostly because the alternatives are impossible to police. However, local planning and nuisance laws make it all but impossible for anyone living in an urban or suburban situation to kill their own animals. You will be liable, should you attempt to kill any animal in an urban situation, to heavy fines and possibly orders forbidding you to keep livestock of any kind.

I must say that I would have more sympathy for all this if we had an adequate supply of local abattoirs for public use. They are increasingly difficult to find and, since their set-up is inevitably geared to larger scale slaughter, how on earth would you get them to kill a single chicken?

The flip side to this argument is animal welfare. If I have to drive an animal fifty miles to wait in a yard where the smell of blood and death is all too apparent to my stock, then it would have been better off being killed at home in a couple of seconds rather than go through all that.

What is scary is that there are 70 million of us on these islands and we will have to rely on more and more killed animals from abroad. When the avian flu first broke out we were importing 3000 tonnes of chicken a month into the UK from the Far East. That is a minimum of 3 million chickens killed under who knows what circumstances. Then they have the cheek to try to do away with home slaughter in the UK.

So, because I want disease free meat that has had something of a normal life, I will keep chickens and kill them myself. I will keep dual purpose birds and let them live until their second string of eggs are gone – who cares if they are a little bit tougher to eat than a bird at six weeks old. I will have had some 500 odd eggs from her and any cockerels will have lived long enough to get his leg over – well his wing over at least!

Why? Because I can. Because I simply refuse to believe, however convincing their arguments about everyone needing cheap chicken and economies of scale, that it is right for humans to do this to another species.

Anyway, I digress.

Why it is important to show you are within the law

You will notice some ambiguities in the law. The words 'private consumption' are key in permitting us to kill animals at home for our own food. I don't remember anyone complaining about this in the law – nor is there anything in the press archives that I can find to show anyone tried to modify this to 'and his family.' So be in no doubt that it is an offense to supply any other person with meat that is not health marked, and this health mark is only available from an abattoir.

Your local authority might have by-laws (they frequently do) regarding animal welfare and slaughter, and you would be wise to check this out before you embarked on your own process. People have been prosecuted by local authorities and the penalties are frequently more than financial.

The law dictates in no uncertain terms how an animal is to be killed. It is an offence to cause 'any avoidable pain, excitement or suffering to any animal'. Under The Agriculture (Miscellaneous Provisions) Act 1968 it is an offence to cause any 'unnecessary pain or unnecessary distress' to any animal. This could mean anything! No matter how much love and attention you have lavished on your animal through its life, anyone could suggest that you have caused suffering and, in today's climate, theb person doing the killing would certainly find it difficult to get a fair hearing?
You will also have to be able to show that you have disposed of any waste material in the approved manner. Incineration is the only legal option for the disposal of carcasses, and parts of carcasses, for certain animal waste such as bovine nervous tissue.

Whether you are slaughtering your own animals or sending them to be killed you will still need to understand the laws governing the transport of animals to slaughter, even if you are moving your stock a mile from a far field.

The actual methods allowed

There are only two methods available to you by law to kill your own animals, and we will go into them in detail later. I mention this now because you might decide to go straight to the butchering chapters of the book.

You can stun and bleed the animal so it dies. This usually involves slitting its throat, 'sticking' it in the chest or cutting the carotid arteries in the neck via the beak in the case of chicken.

How to recognize a good stun

This is crucial in making sure the animal is pain free before it is killed. The time between stunning and bleeding should be as short as possible, but you do need to be on your mettle to do it right.

Firstly, teach your animals to go into confined spaces, to be tethered, to be used to unusual situations. It will then know that there are circumstances that may seem strange but it will no get distressed by them.

Be sure in your own mind about the use of the stun equipment. First practice on dead animals so that you know what it feels like and the amount of pressure you will need. Also be decided exactly what you will do if, for some reason, the stun goes wrong. In an abattoir something like 2% of stuns can be unusual. So, statistically speaking, you might kill animals for the rest of your life and not have a problem.

You should be ready to stun the animal again as quickly as possible avoiding any undue rush or panic. Simply reload the device, then prime and fire it in the correct position. Do not shout and flap about if the worst happens; your own life could be in danger from using the equipment without due care and attention. People do things they should not do under ant circumstances such as put a loaded captive bolt stunner under their arms or between their legs or, worse still, in their teeth, or throw it to someone else. Never do these things! Calmly reload, cock and fire in the right place.

If you have done it correctly animal should:

- Collapse immediately
- The hind legs will be extended and stiff.
- The back arched.
- Breathing will stop.
- The eyes will be glazed and it will not blink if touched.
- The tongue will be loose.

Thrashing

An animal – in particular a pig– will thrash about with its legs. This does not mean it is in pain but is due to the fact that the spinal chord is randomly firing neurons. The point to make, though, is that you will have to get out of the way and be very careful when approaching to cut the neck. You should not wait for the thrashing to stop before cutting if at all possible; get yourself behind the animal and kill it before it starts to recover.

Religious slaughter

It is said that the knife used in religious slaughter is so sharp that the animal cannot feel it. Whether you believe this or not is up to you. However, it is not permitted to kill an animal without stunning it for religious purposes unless you are working as a trained person in a registered abattoir. You cannot otherwise kill any animal with a knife without stunning it legally.

The other permitted way of killing is with a free bullet in the field (which doesn't have to be in a field per se). All of the various means of killing are not permitted at home, including anything that causes pain to the animal.
 Chickens are permitted to be killed by dislocation of the neck in small numbers but you can't chop their heads off with an axe without stunning first, and the various pliers based instruments for doing the job are probably illegal in that they can inflict pain on the bird.

Do not take this book as a manual for killing animals. It does give all the information, and something of the feelings you may go through while doing the job but it is one thing to read about driving a car; the actual experience itself needs to be learned over quite a long period of time. So go and get yourself some training if I have not been able to put you off killing your own meat.

Sending to the abattoir

In the 1930s there were over 13,000 slaughterhouses in the UK. By the turn of the millennium there were just over 400, and in the last half dozen years around another hundred have gone to the wall! Around 50 plants process most of the meat to be found in the supermarkets and this leaves around 250 for the rest of us. The official list shows some counties to be served by only one or two establishments, and so you may well have a long way to go in order to get your animals for killed. Large parts of the South of England are without abattoirs and there are none on the Isle of Wight. You might have to book your animals in many weeks before they are ready. Don't expect to simply turn up with an animal which is ready for slaughter.

If you are able to find an establishment that will kill your animals, you will need to plan the operation well in advance. Get to know the abattoir, its slaughtermen and how they work. Also get your animals on site exactly on time so they do not spend long periods waiting. To the best of your ability make the process as easy for them as possible.

You would be well advised to practice the movement of your animals by putting them in various strange surroundings and restraints, so that when the time comes for real they will not get spooked by what is happening to them.

Many abattoirs have gone to the wall because

of costs. Most small businesses have had to pay for extensive changes in the inspection regime demanding both a meat inspector and a vet. These costs will have been passed on to the customer, and, although you might be prepared to pay the higher charges for dispatching your stock, it makes it very difficult to justify the killing of single animals in any business sense.

Chapter Two
Equipment

In order to process your own meat you will need an array of tools that you simply cannot do without. If you send your animals away to be slaughtered and do not stipulate otherwise, the animal will be returned to you already cut up, probably using a special meat band saw. All you need to do is unpack it and freeze, salt and store it. For larger animals you will need a pulley and tackle to lift it off the ground, a way of shaving pigs and, of course, lots of sharp knives.

Captive Bolt

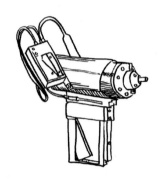

The captive bolt stunner is not designed to kill the animal, although it is lethal to humans If you are going to use one, a captive bolt stunner is an important tool that must be kept in perfect working order, well maintained and kept totally safe. Its use infers a way of restraining the animal because you actually have to place this tool in position on the head of the beast in order for it to work.

Always remember that this is a very dangerous piece of equipment and several things can go wrong with it, particularly when too powerful a cartridge is loaded. Above all, it should be cleaned and checked after each firing and the opportunities for young hands to experiment with it should be avoided at all times. It is definitely not a toy!

Although this book gives proper positioning and instructions for the use of a captive bolt stunner, actually using one for the first time on an animal you have reared yourself can be a very distressing experience. I certainly defy anyone not to be nervous at the very least. Try to get together with someone who has experience of using one, or get yourself some formal training. I have seen many examples of macho use of the stunning gun, and lots of examples of improper use, particularly in relation to not bleeding the animal properly after shooting. To my mind, training and preparation are paramount.

You no longer need a firearms certificate to own one, though its improper use will damage you or not do its job properly or indeed both and, in a worst case scenario, will cause considerable pain and make the animal very, very cross.

There are two kinds of stunner available; a penetrative bolt that enters the brain and a percussive hammer that renders the animal unconscious – most of the time. Once fired, the bolt will automatically retract back into its case.

The percussive type stunner is more difficult to use, particularly on a larger animal. It will frequently fracture the skull, and this is often an indication of a good stun. Clearly, any damage to the brain will release nervous tissue into the bloodstream and there is a playoff between the invasive captive bolt stun which desensitises the animal but keeps the brain stem intact and the desire to reduce the amount of possible BSE material escaping into the meat.

It is most likely that you will use a stunner that takes a cartridge and not the compressed air type. It is important that you use the correct charge for the animal, as detailed in the instructions. Old animals such as an old and fully mature bull are particularly difficult to stun and are probably best dealt with at the abattoir.

If you have a miss-stun you should wait 30 seconds before reloading your cartridge to be sure the charge itself is all used up. Sometimes a second flash can occur.

Important rules

Be calm!

Stunners must always be checked to be safe and unfireable before they are put down.

Do not pass the gun from one person to another when charged and never ever throw it to anyone.

Make sure the stunner us unloaded when moving it from one place to another.

If the bolt does not completely recoil, have the equipment checked.

Do not give another person a loaded stunner.

Be sure the animal is secure in a restraining pen – which will not allow the animal to escape or move. Only stun when you are sure of this.

Clean the equipment after use.

Wear ear and eye protection.

The process of stunning is stun and then bleed. You cannot just assume the animal is dead and delay bleeding. Rest assured that after a proper and successful stun the animal will not feel a thing as you slit its throat.

Stunning hammer

The image of the butcher, a determined look on his face, his muscles taught inside his rolled up sleeves, biting his lip, the sweat forming in beads on his head as he is ready to bash a pig on the head before sticking it in the throat will remain with me forever. I worked as a washer down, which mainly meant that I washed the place with buckets of soapy water after the job was done and, when no one was looking, threw testicles at my cousin (well I thought that's what they were!)

In the UK, the stunning hammer is not mentioned in the law about animal slaughter because it is no longer used, although you can still get them. The law strongly implies that stunning should be done only by a powered instrument, except in the case of poultry and chicks younger than 72 hours old.

Guns

Killing pigeons, rabbits and squirrels can be done with an air rifle, the most powerful kind not needing a firearms licence. Clearly, this is for use only in the wild. Captive rabbits and pigeons are killed by hand. Air rifles should be regularly checked to ensure they give maximum pressure and the pellets actually kill rather than injure. You must not try to kill anything bigger than a rabbit with this weapon. You would have to be the best marksman ever to kill a flying bird with an air rifle and, in order to kill birds in the field, you will need a shotgun. Consequently you will also need a firearms licence for the shotgun and the .22 rifle. It is also strictly illegal to kill an animal with a crossbow bolt or arrow in the United Kingdom.

There are many advantages of killing a large animal with a powerful gun. First of all, you are more or less sure it is dead without having to actually touch it with the captive bolt. In order to use a captive bolt properly the animal really needs to be restrained because there is a good chance it will be spooked by the gun itself.

Using a free bullet you can see the animal eating and behaving normally and then kill it instantly without it knowing a thing. The law in the UK stipulates that when using a free bullet in the field, you must be certain that the exit of the bullet will not hit anyone. Clearly this has both targeting and ricochet implications. A .22 bullet coming out of a cow's head will still be deadly for a further half a mile and consequently should only be fired into a hill or some other absorbent material.

Firing a shotgun into an animal's head from around 30cm will create an entry hole but the pellets are unlikely to escape the skull. Therefore you are able to shoot the animal in a more enclosed situation, but you still have to be careful to consider the possibility that some pellets may become free.

UK law does not cater for the use of shotguns to kill large captive animals. A number of local authorities do provide advice on this technique though. I have to say the sight of an animal with a hole in its head pumping blood is not pleasant one.

Although we will mention it again later, even if you have shot an animal in the head it should still be bled. Once you have shot the beast you should slit its throat from ear to ear as far back as the bone. This process guarantees death within a very few seconds. The animal shot in the head can and does rally somewhat, gains consciousness and groans. The stunned animal will feel no pain as you slit its throat – that's why you stun it! Get it straight, an animal larger than a rabbit has to be bled, so either get used to it or keep something else, or use the abattoir.

Knives

You can get by with a big knife and a small knife. More properly you will need a boning knife which is small and allows you to get every bit of meat from the bone. A boning knife has a curved blade to present a cutting surface at various angles. A fillet knife has a flat blade for slicing straight. A large butcher's knife is like a big boning knife in that it has a curved blade. If you are starting afresh, a good set

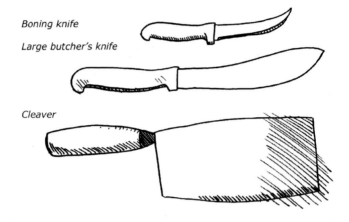

Boning knife

Large butcher's knife

Cleaver

of butchers knives will cost a small fortune, but will be worth every penny and should last a lifetime.

Cleavers are good for chopping large amounts of muscle, but are really there for breaking through bones, particularly ribs. You can get a good cleaver from the Chinese supermarket these days at a fraction of the price you might pay at a butcher's supplier. They illustrate the difference between chopping and cutting. Chopping actually cuts in two ways. Firstly it forces molecules to fall onto either side of the blade, thus giving two pieces. It also creates a fault line in a material such as a bone, which then cracks or splits along that line. This way you can pare down bones to remove the marrow, which I feed to the dog. In effect it is the butcher's version of the billhook and you use the flat of the blade to part the bone.

The other way of dealing with bones is to saw them, and for this you need a meat saw. Cleavers work

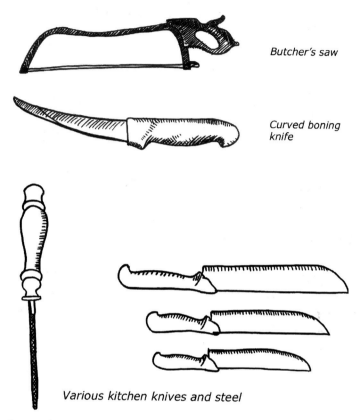

Butcher's saw

Curved boning knife

Various kitchen knives and steel

best along the grain, saws against it. At a pinch you can get by with a large clean hacksaw but a real meat saw is the best option. A fine hacksaw blade clogs up too much and you are forever cleaning it, and new ones have blue dyes on them which I have learnt to my cost.

Sharpening knives

Oh! What a can of worms. It seems that everyone

Buckets of water and gloves

has become a 'Ray Mears' these days and there is a huge collection of good, bad and indifferent information out there. The most important piece of equipment, no matter how good your knives are, is a stone and steel. The stone makes the edge and the steel hones it. Without a sharp knife you might as well hack the thing to bits with your granny's false teeth, assuming you can find them.

You will need a wet stone that takes away the rough metal and creates the edge. If you angle your knife too high the bevel will become too flat and the knife will become blunt. After just a few sharpenings like this your knife will decrease in sharpness each time.

Hold your knife at a 25 degree angle, as though you are going to cut a thin slice out of the stone and press reasonably firmly as you draw the knife forwards over it. Then reverse it. Resist the temptation to lift the knife so it feels as though it is biting.

Then hone it with the steel. A real razor uses a strop of leather. All the steel or strop does is take off the tiny imperfections and you do not press hard – especially with steel. You'll just take the edge off if you do.

Hand in glove

A carcass, particularly a beef carcass, that has been allowed to cool, often in very cold conditions, is alarmingly cold on the hands. You should expect the hands to be cold and so they should be; it helps to keep infections down. You should have a good supply of surgical gloves to maintain this process and, if you are as clumsy as I am, I would buy a butcher's metal glove. You only need one; for the left hand if you are right handed and visa versa.

Table

A butcher's table is about two feet thick and is gradually worn away over the years to about six inches. You don't really need a butcher's table but you do need something really substantial for a number of reasons. Firstly, you are not cutting up the odd mushroom here. This is meat and sometimes you have to work with forces and instruments that resemble the House of Horrors. The last thing you need is the table to disintegrate beneath a swift blow with the cleaver, or to shoot across the kitchen.

Secondly, the table has to be cleaned, both before and after the operation. If you can get a good quality second table then all the better, but most of us have to eat off the table we cut on, so it has to be able to take a good scrubbing brush.

I have found that Formica (or whatever it is called these days) is no good because, no matter how careful I am, I will cut through the material into the wood beneath. (I tend to do this even when making a sandwich though!) This cut line will now be a source of infection forever, no matter how much I clean it.

Block and tackle

You might be a giant and able to hold a pig by its back legs while your partner cleans it out, but I'm not. Neither is it good practice to dissect the animal on the floor. The instructions in this book assume you can hoist the animal. This also infers that the block and tackle is fixed properly, and the building it is set in can also take the weight. This may seem obvious to you but my great uncle tried to do the job in an adapted Anderson Shelter just after the Second World War and brought the lot down on himself. (He thought he could make some money selling pig meat but went to prison instead).

Restraint

If you are going to use a captive bolt stunning gun you really need to work out a way of restraining the animal. This should go hand in hand with training the animal during its lifetime to go calmly into restraining equipment. The motto of this book is that slaughter begins at birth, and here's the reason why: you are constantly working towards the day when the animal will be killed for food, unless it is a pet. Restraints should be such that the animal can be lifted easily from the killing area on a block and tackle, and the restraint removed. Of course, all this is not needed if you shoot the animal in the head.

Devices for killing poultry

You will notice that the law does not specify any devices for killing poultry. You can buy inverted killing tubes where you turn the bird upside down and stuff it in what looks like a traffic cone, so its head peeps out of the bottom. You can also buy special pliers that allow you to break its neck or a device with a 'v' shaped hole in a piece of broom so that you can trap the head underneath and pull. All of these are, to my mind, unnecessary and will probably inflict various amounts of pain or distress.

Chapter Three
Beef

You will need a serious amount of help in order to butcher a cow. You might find that a bullet from a .22 rifle simply makes the animal angry. You are not going to lift the beast to get the skin off on your own and, in the long run, you will have to think long and hard about whether it isn't better to take the animal to the abattoir. But then, if you live in an English county where there are no facilities, you are faced with a horrid dilemma. Convenience verses animal welfare. For me, animal welfare will always win out, and if you are able to do it – get it done. But planning is important.

There is so much of a beef animal, whether it is a young steer or a ten year old milk cow who has given a hundred thousand gallons of milk over the years.The insides of a beef animal are rudely voluminous and they will shock you as they fall. The dead animal can be almost as heavy as a car engine and the heart itself can be as large as your head. The bladder is enormous and you could make a sleeping bag out of its stomachs. The amount of blood you get pouring from the slit animal is enough to drown in.

If you are considering keeping cattle for personal meat and thinking of killing it yourself, you will certainly have quite a job on your hands.

You will also need to be sure that you can eat and salt and freeze all this meat and that you have a room big enough to actually do the job of cutting it up. Remember, it is against the law to share the meat out around the village or to swap it for a bit of pork or lamb. It is all yours an must be consumed by you!

It is really important that you find someone who has done this many times before and learn from them. It is impossible to kill and butcher cattle with this book in one hand and a humane stunner in the other. This chapter is only a guide to killing cattle. It us up to you to get the necessary experience. It can be successfully argued that to kill an ox without experience borders on the criminal.

If you are at all in doubt about this operation, take the beast to the slaughterhouse.

What you will need

Plenty of water for cleaning.
Surgical rubber gloves.
A couple of knives and a steel.
A long knife for cutting the neck.
A sharp chopper.
A meat saw.
A hat.
A captive bolt stunner
Restraining equipment.
Clean receptacles – big ones!

You will probably also need a hook and possibly a block and tackle and a small crowd to help you lift the animal. If you only have ropes and tackle you will need a tractor to lift the animal and an extra way of securing it in position so it doesn't fall. It is worth mentioning again that you must make sure your building can take the weight and do not rely on using something like a tractor to keep it in place.

There would be little use in starving the animal; it would take such a long time for the food to be removed from the animal that it would be inconsiderate to do so. The animal needs to be in a very clean shed with a strong beam for lifting, plenty of water for washing and at least a tap to which a hose can be attached and a drain through

The stunning point

which liquids can escape.

The animal needs to be restrained in order to fall without injuring people or breaking equipment. The animal is stunned at the cross point of the horns and the eyes. Once stunned the animal will fall and its neck should be cut so that both carotid arteries are severed and the animal bleeds.

Note: The animal might well be killed away from where it is butchered and you will need a tractor to move the carcass from one place to another.

Hoisting

Skin the legs and hook each at the hock. You can then saw off the feet, but not too near to the hock because the tendon might give. Lift the animal's back end off the floor a little and doubly secure the legs with rope. You do not want it falling on you.

Now wash your hands.

Skinning

Carefully cut, knife blade uppermost, from the inside of each leg to the anus which you should dissect out and tie securely with good string. The more frequently you wash your hands from now on, the better the meat will be. Bits of hair will adhere to the meat and are very difficult to remove, so take your time and be very careful.

Cut the skin from the breastbone in a line and then take a saw to split the breastbone. The front end of the animal is still on the floor. Forward of the udder area, cut into the midline of the belly and carefully cut the skin with the blade outermost so that the intestines are not troubled. This cut is going to join with the cut at the breastbone.

Remove the head and cut the skin on the forelegs, which can then also be removed. You can pull off the skin rather like a pullover, leaving it on the rump as a protection.

Go behind the animal and slit its throat to the bone

The anus has already been cut out so you can find it and draw out all the intestines. You might need to cut out parts where they are connected to the body cavity but it should all fall quite easily. Cut round the diaphragm and pull out the top of the gullet, which can be tied off first to avoid spillage.

Once the guts have fallen, get them out of the way. You might find it easier to remove the liver before you cut the diaphragm, and remove the gall bladder before it bursts its contents onto your meat.

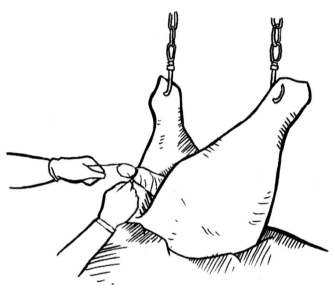

Tie of the anus

You will need to spread the thorax, probably with a stick to enable you to get the pluck out.

Down the other end you will need to dissect the udder and the penis or the uterus, the bladder and associated connective tissue. This is surprisingly hard work. Make sure that you do not puncture anything!

Keep the kidneys and the liver, dissect the tongue and keep the pancreas. You can make tripe from the paunch.

Finally, remove the skin and wash the carcass with

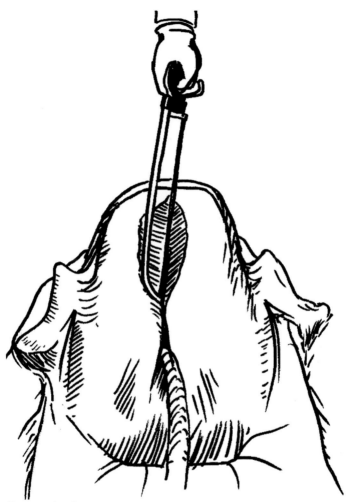

Opening the chest cavity

a hose-pipe, making sure that everything else has been cleared away.

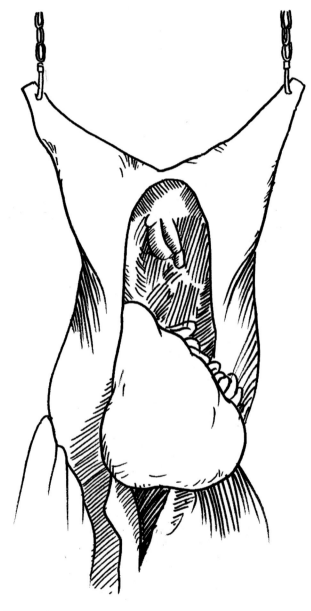

Pulling out the gut

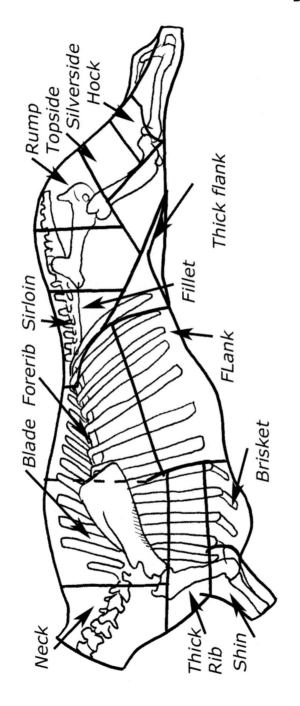

Butchering Beef

In the EU the law says that all cattle older than 12 months have to have their backbones removed at an approved site. In the UK we do not have to do this because we have the over 30 months scheme (OTM) and have agreed that our backbones can remain. However, the OTM scheme is coming to an end and there are moves to unify what happens across Europe. It is likely that all cattle over 24 months will have to have their backbones removed at an approved abattoir.

This means that the keeping of cattle in a small herd will probably no longer be feasible and you wouldn't be able to butcher your own beef because of the economics of growing young beef. You will also not be able to kill and eat your old milker so if you were wondering about being free after the end of the OTM scheme, forget it! These plans may also put an end to T-bone steaks.

You may by now be sick of reading this but....

Butchering a carcass of beef is a huge undertaking. Each quarter will probably weigh more than you do, even if you chop up one of your Jerseys that won't give you brilliant meat anyway, and it will certainly take ages. You will need a table that can take the weight and you will also need help lifting it onto the table. THEN you will have to deal with the meat once you have chopped it up. And before this there is the question of hanging it.

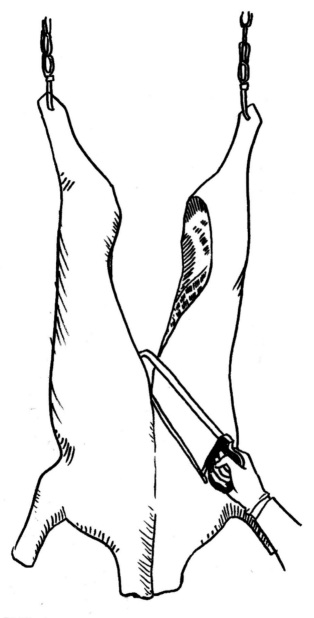

Dividing into two

Alternatively, you could get the animal to a pre-arranged appointment at the abattoir and have them chop the carcass into manageable pieces for you – or, if you like, to even butcher the entire carcass.

You can hang your meat for up to ten days to permit the enzymes and bacteria to make it less tough. I always worry about this – in my student days, lectures on microbiology always made me more interested in cutting down unknown bacterial growth.

Tie the head to a beam so that it doesn't fall on you as you cut the spare flesh with a knife and then with a saw. There is certainly a lot of meat on a beef head so don't waste it.

Next saw down the backbone. You can use an axe, but you are more likely to mess it up that way. You can also use a power saw but you are more likely to cut yourself up with it. I'd stick to slow and steady if I was you. It is hard work, but you should end up with two halves, each of which will need to be transported to the table

Find the last rib and make a cut at the end of the meat to serve as a marker. Then, using a boning knife where possible and the saw when necessary, cut the half into two by separating this last rib from the rest and sawing through the backbone.

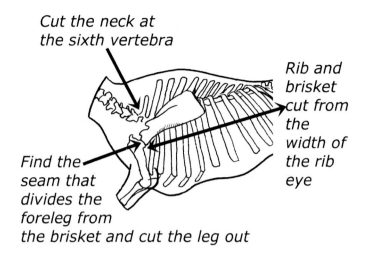

Cut the neck at the sixth vertebra

Rib and brisket cut from the width of the rib eye

Find the seam that divides the foreleg from the brisket and cut the leg out

A rolled neck joint - at least 3 - probably better with 5 ties

Forequarter

Neck

Place the forequarter skin down and cut through the backbone directly after the sixth vertebra from the neck. Then, after some hard work, use a large knife to cut through the flesh that is parallel to the arm bone. You should aim to get the leg out at the ball and socket joint, which you can cut through with the large knife. The neck should then fall away. You can help this by using the boning knife if necessary. The neck end can be boned and trimmed, then rolled, but I prefer to cube the meat for stewing. If you want steaks then

55

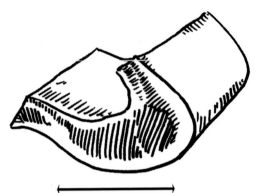

The length of the rib eye to measure rib and brisket cut

you will have to trim out all the fat.

Brisket 'leg of mutton' joint

The front of the brisket is a large muscle that powers the foreleg and can be removed by finding the natural seam between the muscle of the leg and the rest of the brisket. Pare away using the boning knife and the muscle will come away. This can be neatly trimmed and cut into steaks.

Forerib and brisket

If you look towards the backbone end of the forequarter you will see the ribeye muscle that looks like some bacon. Measure this across and mark the rib at half that distance further in from the tip of the eye. On the other end, mark where the ball and socket joint ends. Turn the forequarter over and join up the two marks. Next, cut with a knife and saw to

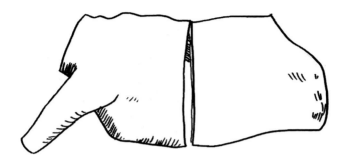

Dividing the forequarter at the shoulder

separate the forerib from the brisket.

Trim the fat from the brisket along with the connective tissue. Then use the boning knife to pare away the bone from the meat. There is a lot of fat and many small muscles here which you should keep. Cut out the sternum and all the ribs together. You can remove the meat from the ribs at a later stage.

Trim away at everything so that you have a lean cut. Divide the sheet of meat into two equal pieces lengthways and then roll and tie each joint. This can easily be sliced into three joints, so that you get six in total from the whole animal.

Remove the ribs and the backbone in a single piece with the boning knife to release the forerib meat. Remove the gristle and fat from the back and the bottom of the meat. You will find that there are many small muscles all over the place that can also be trimmed out and kept.

This can now be rolled and tied and cut to make the correct sized joint.

Rib steaks

Cut the bone completely out of the fore rib. You will find a number of muscles here. The meat between the ribs can be cut out with the boning knife. The rib eye is a muscle that has a natural joint between the meat below it. Pare this away with the boning knife and fingers and remove completely.

The scraggier piece of meat can be trimmed, rolled and tied to make a rib joint.

Hindquarter

On the hip there is a big piece of fat which marks the flap of flesh and the line of fat that is the flank. Cut and pare away at the fat until you get to the top of the hip bone. Then make a line from a point a few centimetres in from the eye muscle at the other end, just as was done on the forequarter. Now cut through it with a knife and saw.

You now have the thin flank removed.

Fillet

Under the hip and the backbone you will find a muscle. Pare away with the boning knife on the hip

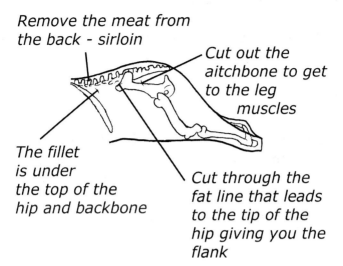

Remove the meat from the back - sirloin

Cut out the aitchbone to get to the leg muscles

The fillet is under the top of the hip and backbone

Cut through the fat line that leads to the tip of the hip giving you the flank

and then work along the contours of the backbone. Keep the knife bone side so that you don't cut the muscle. Trim the fillet of fat and the raggedy bits. It can be rolled or cut into steaks.

Sirloin

This is the muscle on the back. Find the bottom vertebra and saw through it. Use the boning knife to take the muscle from the backbone and ribs. The meat between the ribs can be taken out for mincing.

Trim the sirloin of fat and gristle and this can either be tied or used as steaks. There is a line of fat at the bottom of the sirloin which, if you remove it, allows you to roll the joint more easily. Once tied, you can roll it or cut it into steaks.

Rump

This is mainly the meat around the hip. The hip forms a G clamp shape and the pubic bone should be prominent at the lower end. About a third or so up from this, make a cut with a saw and a knife through the hip. This will separate the rump from the rest of the hindquarter, now called the topbit.

Hock

Find the kneecap and cut underneath it into the joint with a large knife. Once on the other side, cut at a 45 degree angle downwards to release the lower leg or hock. The joint might need a little work and you may need to use a saw.

Topside

Remove the aitchbone which has a lot of meat on it, particularly in the hole of the hip. Work around the bone with the paring knife and you will eventually find the ball and socket. Pull hard on the aitchbone to get more access. You may find you need help to do this.

To remove the topside look for two layers of fat between the three muscles of the upper leg. The first one is the topside, which you pare away with a small knife in order to get the muscle free.

In doing so you will hit the femur at the half way point. Continue on beyond it. Trim off the fat in order to get the whole muscle free. Then trim the fat from the meat.

Silverside and thick flank

To get this muscle free you will need to pare out the femur, which you can do with the boning knife. You will remember also that the kneebone was left behind, so this will also need to be cut out.

Now find the natural joint between the silverside and the thick flank. Pare it away and, once removed, you can trim both joints. You can then tie them up or cut them up for steaks.

Chapter Four
Venison

I often find it surprising that some people who hunt or shoot venison feel they need to make excuses for what they are doing. They talk of culling and keeping the population in check, of 'maintaining the genetic fitness' of the herd or of keeping the correct age distribution.

In the United States there is a hunting season when people simply go out to hunt the deer because they like venison; end of story! In my view, if it is right that we eat these animals then we should not have to make any other excuses other than that we do the killing in a completely humanely manner.

In truth, this chapter is here for completeness. Deer are the happiest of all food animals because they are eating one second but not the next. Alive and aware of their surroundings one second and then, completely pain free, dead the next.

In order to shoot deer you will need considerable skill and training and this includes the cleaning of the animal in the field. You will certainly learn what to do far easier from an experienced practitioner than from any book although the written word will give you the basic grounding.

There are many regulations regarding the killing of deer. In the UK the law was changed in 2007 and you should make yourself aware of these changes and how they affect you. In particular, the use of .220 ammunition is only permissible if you are killing smaller deer such as muntjac and Chinese Water deer. For these animals you will also need a muzzle energy of not less than 1000 foot pounds and you should use a soft or hollow nosed bullet weighing not less than 50 grains.

Everything else should be killed with a rifle with a calibre no less than .240 inches, a muzzle energy of not less than 1700 ft lbs and a soft or hollow nosed bullet. Also, deer should not be killed with shotguns.

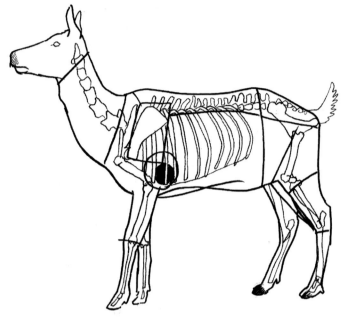

The shot to kill a deer is at the heart

Kill shot

The kill shot is into the heart and the aiming point is just behind the shoulder, where death will be instantaneous. You will probably be firing from up a tree or on a platform and, although this is not a hunting book, you should only fire when you are sure your bullet will go into the earth behind the animal because it will remain lethal for quite a distance once it has left the animal.

Once certain that the animal is dead, you will need to get the heat out of it, and this will require the removal of its insides.

Dressing

Wear rubber gloves and work quickly and methodically. You will need a sharp knife and your first job is to cut round the anus, or vulva if female. Pull the anus out a little and tie it off so that there is no leakage.

You are going to cut from the breastbone with the blade uppermost so that you do not cut the intestines all the way down the belly to the bottom of your first cut.

The stomach can be eased out and tied off at the gullet to stop any leakage. You can cut here to release the stomach and work your hand inside, pulling and releasing the intestines from their connective tissue.

Once outside, the guts can be put away or wrapped up for removal. The pelvic area will still have glands associated with it and you should use your knife to clean out everything, including the prostrate and any seminal glands still there. The bladder should have come out with the gut if you cut round the vulva or penis.

You can cut out the diaphragm and slice the neck through to the bone to allow you to pull out the pluck. Keeping the heart. Alternatively, put your knife under the breastbone and pull, so that the chest is opened and you can then dissect the pluck and the rest of the gullet.

Some people take the kidneys out at this stage and place them with the heart and liver. The deer has no gallbladder. Others choose to leave them stuck to the back wall of the animal. In any case, get your animal back home as soon as you can and hang it by the hock as you would with other animals. It should hang in a cool room overnight, but first give the carcass a good wash with plenty of cold water.

Skinning

Deer hair can be a serious pain if it gets onto the meat because you will almost need microsurgery to get it off again, so always cut outwards from inside. The animal is hanging by the back legs, so ring the legs carefully near the hock. Then cut up the inside of the leg to meet the belly line cut you made in the field.

Do also remember to wash your hands frequently during this process.

Next you are going to fist the skin away, like a sheep. It should come away quite easily, but avoid touching the white flash of fur that is strong smelling. If you do touch it, wash and wash again!

I also choose to remove the tail for the simple reason that it is easier than slitting the skin off.

You should be able to pull down the skin rather like a pullover down to the shoulders. (I often think of this when playing rugby because I invariably need

Sever the neck as close to the body as possible

help to get my sweaty shirt off!)

Treat the forelegs exactly as the rear, cutting into the armpits. You are more likely to find blood pools that have clotted at this end. Use plenty of water and do take your time to wash it out. Peel the skin back to the neck and stop.

I have heard of many different ways of continuing here but none are from my own experience as I personally have no interest in making a trophy of the animal's head. I have no time for that sort of thing. If you have not already severed the neck in

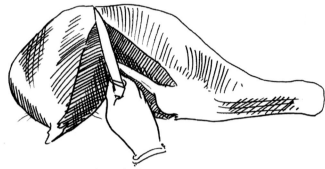

Removing the rump from the leg

the field, you will need to do so now. I use a chopper, but a saw will do just as well.

Now wash everything again with copious amounts of water and clean up ready for quartering.

(It's both puzzling and funny how words get into the hunting vocabulary but not into farming. Quartering happens to all game animals, not butchering. Dogs also quarter in the field, but here it means to work round one section before moving onto the next!)

Notes on butchering venison

What you won't find much of in a deer is fat. Indeed, it is at a premium, and this makes venison the best of red meats. Many recipes actually go on about putting fat into the meat.

On the whole, deer are generally treated as lamb. The cuts are described below, but you can decide to ignore them as you feel fit. In particular, people

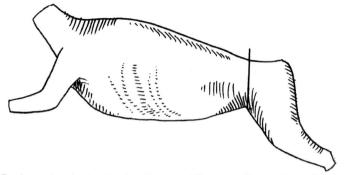

For home butchering the deer is treated like lamb. Cut the legs off at the hip, divide and remove the rump

often decide they prefer venison steaks, and consequently they do not tie the meat for joints. All the boned material can be diced for stews and pies. Stow pie is probably one of the finest things you could possibly ever bite into!

If you read through the beef and lamb butchering sections you will have enough information to produce the various cuts you need.

Flank

Flank meat is used for stewing and pies, cut clear from the ribcage and chopped.

Haunch

This is the leg muscle and you get to it in precisely the same way as you do in lamb. Although the same muscles as in topside, silverside and thick end are found in deer, they are small and are not separated out. When you cut the knuckle out, keep the bones

– indeed keep all of the bones – for making stock.

Neck

Bone out as in lamb and use it for stews etc.

Saddle (Rack and Loin)

The rack is the front half of the saddle, the loin is the rear. Cut out the eye muscle for medallions.

This is another more expensive prime cut and is where fillet and medallions are cut from. The front part is called the rack and is suitable for dry heat cooking such as roasting or grilling.

The fillet is the underside and should be removed as for lamb. The loins should be cut out with the boning knife and rolled and tied for joints, or may be cut for steaks.

Shank

This should be boned away and used for stews.

Shoulder

You can pare away at the shoulder meat as you would for lamb, either by cutting the shoulder into two halves using the saw, or by simply moving your way round the back of the shoulder. Each half can then be rolled and tied or chopped for stewing meat.

Chapter Five
Pork

You can eat everything but the squeal, which is sold to British Leyland Trucks for the brakes.

The pig is a wonderful animal. It is keen, intelligent and certainly wonderful to eat! It is their intelligence that makes them so difficult to kill, to my mind at least, since they seem to understand so much. One of the greatest conversations I ever had was with a pig.

For me (and this is probably why I shall never run the world!) each home would have a quarter of an acre around it; there is plenty of space even if there are 70 million of us. And each plot would have a pig in it. As John Seymour said, we'd all be much happier, healthier and understanding people. Ah well.. dreams is dreams and sadly will probably remain as such!

To kill a pig is the mainstay of self-sufficiency. Possibly it is the next step up from chickens but the big problem you will encounter is most likely falling in love with them. On the other hand, pigs are willful and creatures of habit. If you try to withdraw food prior to killing it, the pig might get angry and it is certainly plenty big enough to break down any structure you may care to keep it in.

What you will need

Plenty of water for cleaning.
Surgical rubber gloves.
A couple of knives and a steel including a long boning knife for cutting the neck.
A sharp chopper.
A meat saw.
A hook and possibly a block and tackle – or certainly someone to help you lift the animal.
A captive bolt stunner or a .22 rifle (for use in a position where there is no chance of a ricochet)
Possibly a saw rack.
Restraining equipment.
Clean receptacles.

A blowtorch for removing the hair and bristles.

A good scraping knife.

Stunning

If you are going to use a captive bolt stunner, the animal will have to be tethered and restrained, which is more easier said than done. The point of contact is that cross line from ears to eyes. The same goes for shooting it with a .22 bullet.

Stunning point

Killing

The stuck method uses a long bladed boning knife. Within seconds of the animal

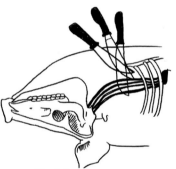

The killing stroke of the knife

being stunned it is rolled over and the long blade is pushed into the neck below the breastbone, the sharp point facing downwards.

Using the breastbone as a fulcrum, the blade handle is thrust forwards, pushing the cutting edge of the knife through the heart. Moving the blade from side to side inside the chest cavity will cut the aorta. You can also sever the carotid arteries in the neck

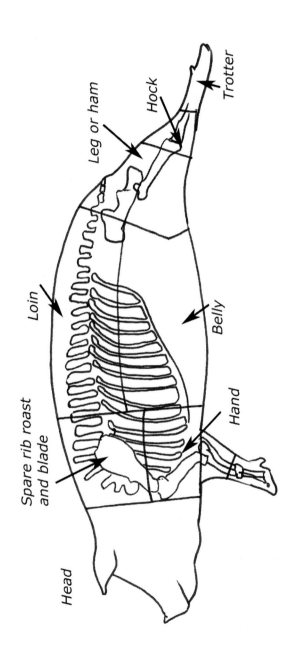

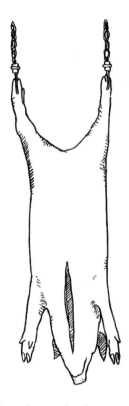

Slit and cut at the chest

at the same time. Within 30 seconds the animal will be dead.

Lifting

Hook the hind legs at the hock as with other animals and lift it with a block and tackle. I have done it this way because, in the end, it (well I think so anyway) is less effort. Bristles are the enemy of great pork, so they have to be removed. Some people shave the beast, some put it in straw and burn it, some scald the pig in a barrel of hot water and shave it but I simply burn them all off using a blowtorch. This is more easily done with the animal raised. This process can blacken the skin but this can then be scraped to make it more 'pig' coloured.

Now wash your hands.

Cut from the sticking point forwards towards the chin and locate the gullet and windpipe. The windpipe is reinforced. Tie off the gullet with string just to aid against spillage, and also cut out the tongue for later use, keeping it in a clean container.

75

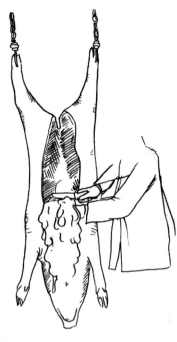

Cleaning out the gut

You can remove the head at this point. You may actually choose to remove the head once the pig is stunned if you prefer, and dissect the tongue later. Alternatively you might even choose to leave the head on and split it with the rest of the carcass. The brain is certainly edible, just not by me.

Split the breastbone with the meat saw and then cut round the anus, tying it off with string to avoid spillage. Cut around the penis or vagina area and make a slit, blade uppermost, along the mid line of the animal to join the slit breastbone.

Now wash your hands.

Place a hand inside and carefully pull out the intestines into the receptacle you have provided for the job. The bladder should come away with its associated organs, though you might have to help with any connective tissue in order to remove the uterus (if female).

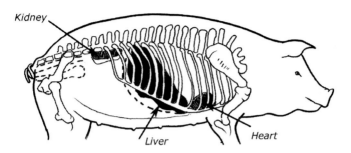

You might have to cut round the diaphragm and, once through, the stomach and gullet should fall easily.

The liver should stay intact, from which you should carefully remove the bile duct which, if broken, will ruin the meat. Recover the kidneys and set them aside with the liver. Pull open the chest cavity and draw out the pluck; both heart and lungs.

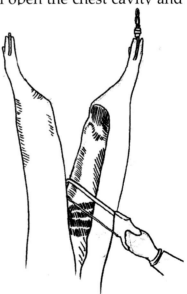

Now wash the whole pig, both inside and out.

Dividing

You can slice from the tail end to the pelvis and then, using a meat saw, cut down the backbone. You can continue this process with a chopper if you prefer, so you will now

Divide the cleaned pig into two halves

77

have two halves ready for butchering. Leave these halves ready for butchering the following day, but clear away the mess and incinerate it.

It is true that you can wash out the intestines for sausage making. They are turned inside out and scraped to remove everything, along with the soft lining of the intestine. They can then be packed in salt and stored, but, as we said for sheep – they can be easily bought.

The headmeat is used for brawn
The feet are used to make gelatine
The tial is roasted
The pluck and liver make pate
The pancreas is fried and eaten
The kidneys and liver are fried
The uterus is cooked in Chinese recipes
The bladder is blown up and played with

Butchering a pig

For this operation you will do well to wear a decent apron made of heavy cotton.

Pork is a fresh and sweet meat that does not have to be hung at all. In fact hanging it is not advised at all. Simply allow the carcass to cool overnight and the following day you can begin the task of cutting.

As ever, we start with controversy. Most people remove the head at this point, using a saw to cut through the vertebrae. Some people simply saw through the backbone to cut the animal in two, splitting the head in the process, but this is a gory job I have never done it myself, though I did see it done in the abattoir as a youth.

I have never roasted the head and put an apple in its mouth as you sometimes see in the movies. To me this seems a silly thing to do, but I have pulled the meat off the bone with a boning knife and made brawn, which is perhaps one of the best things you can have on a sandwich.

Brawn

To make brawn you must slowly simmer the head in a large pan until the skin and meat fall off, adding more boiling water as the liquid evaporates and skimming the scum off as it forms. Add some whole onions cut in half and some carrots chopped into large chunks for good measure.

Remove all the bits from the liquor and reduce it by 75%. Meanwhile, pull off all the meat from all over the head and set it into a clean dish. Lightly salt and pepper it with 15 grams of salt if it has to keep for any length of time. It certainly never has in our house.

Finally, pour the liquor over the meat through a muslin cloth so it just covers the whole and allow it to set.

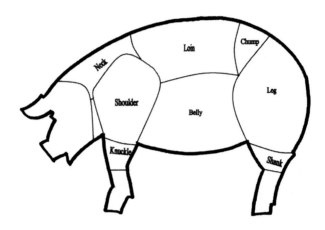

Splitting

Make a cut at the top of the animal and use a meat saw to cut down the backbone. Once you can get a cleaver in, you can work down with this. Carefully and slowly cut down the centre until you are left with two halves of pig.

Believe me, carrying half a carcass of pig is no mean feat so why not get the wife to do it! It should now be taken it to its final cutting place which, again, should be a very sturdy table.

For our purposes the pig will be divided into three:

Leg and Chump

The leg and chump is cut between the last and the next to last vertebra before the pelvis. Zoologists

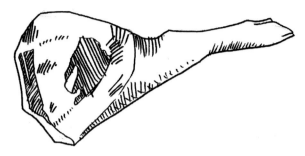

The ham, hock and trotter

call these the lumbar vertebrae, and there are five of them. You are cutting between number four and five. Some butchers mistakenly refer to them as the first and second. The carcass should be placed skin down on the table. You might find the breast bone gets in the way at the bottom of the cut. All you need is a s large sharp knife. If you push the knife through the inter-vertrebral disc, then you won't need a saw.

To remove the leg from the chump you are cutting from the bottom end of the pelvis, the pubic bone, about three fingers towards the chump. Start with the knife, then cut through the bone with the saw, but finish the job with the knife again. Do not try to cut through the flesh with a saw. Give the cut a wash to remove any bits of bone.

Remove the trotters at the heel, if you haven't already done so, and then cut out the aitchbone with the boning knife. You will find this on the meat side of the cut, covered in a small piece of muscle.

shoulder

Front Forequarter

Simply work the boning knife all the way around the bone, keeping the blade as flat as you can for most of the time. The boning knife is easier to use in the reverse position, with the blade actually facing you. The aitchbone actually has the 'ball and socket' joint in it, so you will effectively be cutting the leg bone free from the hip.

Trim the joint so that loose pieces of muscle can be cut away and large acreages of fat can also be removed. Keep the trimmings either for rendering or mincing.

Once the leg is trimmed, tie it up. Every couple of centimetres tie a loop of butcher's string quite tightly round it, pulling the skin side round as much as possible. Tie reasonably tightly, but not so much as to embed the string in the meat. You will need up to eight pieces of string.

Now you can simply cut the joint up into the various cuts you prefer, using a knife and a saw.

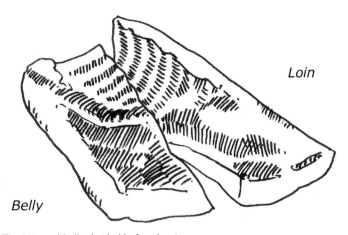

The loin and belly divided before boning

If you want to make a ham, do not tie the meat. Remove as much of the fat as you can. I always score mine skin side so that the cure can get inside to the actual meat where it is needed. The more you trim the meat, the better your final ham will look.

Fore end

To remove the shoulder, cut between the forth and the fifth thoracic ribs. Just count them down from the neck and use a saw to cut through the backbone and the breastbone, finishing off with a large knife. Remove the trotter at what looks like a knee joint.

Divide the shoulder into two not so equal halves by cutting through where the backbone overhangs. Then you can remove the 'spare ribs ' from the leg side using the boning knife and trim the joint as much as possible before tying it as above.

The other half of the joint contains the backbone and the sacrum, or shoulder bone. This last bone should be cut out with the boning knife and then trimmed and tied up. It is called the spare rib roasting joint.

Middle

This is what you will be left with after you have taken the fore end and the chump and leg.

The fillet is inside the back of the animal. Trim away at the flesh, fat and any glands and if you haven't already done so, remove the kidney. Trim out the muscle attached to the backbone and the inner body cavity. Use a boning knife and keep it as flat as possible. Working slowly the 40cm long muscle should come away quite easily. Then trim the loin of fat, again keeping the blade flat.

The meat is then divided into two, lengthways to give you the belly and the loin.

The loin side of the joint has a large muscle that looks like the bacon muscle on a back rasher and is called the 'eye' muscle. This is surrounded at the bottom by rib. The cut along the ribs is made at the width of the 'eye' muscle from the rib and goes all the way down the centre of the carcass. Saw where necessary, but cut everywhere else with a knife.

You now should have a loin end and a belly end.

The loin is cut away from the backbone and half

ribs with the boning knife. You can remove the skin and the outer fat or simply keep it if you wish. You can now choose either to make loin steaks by slicing or you can make back bacon.

The belly end invariably has a lot of fat on it, and this can be removed before removing the breastbone with the boning knife. You will have to cut through the cartilage and then pare away at the flesh against the ribs to remove them completely. This is a sheet of rib ends. They are superb cured, but can also be used as spare ribs.

Clean the belly of any excessive fat and any connective tissue. I also like to remove the teats (perhaps they make me sad) by slicing this amount of skin away.

The whole joint is then rolled up and tied. The joint can then either be sliced and cured as bacon untied or sliced up to provide joints.

To get the best crackling I recommend that you score the skin.

Chapter Six
Lamb, Mutton and Goat

Lambs have their birthday on January 1st when they become mutton, and to my mind the meat is so much better when they are around 18 months old. Most lamb is killed at around the age of 10 months, sometimes even younger. The problem for me is that feeding a large family with a small leg isn't enough and I like to have enough left over for a sandwich because there is nothing so wonderful as lamb (or mutton) on bread and butter with a little salt. As you can see, I am something of a fan.

I have a great deal of sympathy with the view that there is no point in keeping sheep in small numbers because they can be such troublesome animals. They seem to have an in-built capacity for dying, whether by drowning, simply getting lost or getting run over. They tend to mess their rear ends and consequently represent a wonderful attraction to every insect on the planet, they get sick and need almost constant treatment and, to top it all, it costs you more to shear its coat than the thing is worth.

Now, although my publisher will not agree with this statement, I am not interested in money at all, and so I wouldn't mind swapping a couple of pigs for a couple of lambs (or whatever the bartering system exchange rate might be). The whole system of keeping sheep is better when you have a fair few of them. It also has to be said that British sheep (lamb or mutton) are superior to anything in the world. It's because we have the best grass in the world, produced by the most favourable climate.

Preparation

The animal should be killed in cold conditions if possible, and kept in a clean, dry pen for 24 hours prior to the job, with no food but plenty of water. Try to keep the wool clean and do not allow the animal access to any others.

What you will need

Plenty of water for cleaning

Surgical rubber gloves
A couple of knives (one a long boning knife for cutting the neck) and a steel
A sharp chopper.
A meat saw.
A hook and possibly a block and tackle, or someone to help you lift the animal.
A captive bolt stunner.
Possibly a saw rack.
Restraining equipment.
Clean receptacles.

Stunning point

The animal should be killed by slitting the throat, having first been stunned. Draw an imaginary cross-line between the ears and the eyes. This is your aiming point. Of course the animal's head will have to be restrained if you are using a captive bolt tool.

Within seconds of stunning, insert the boning knife into the neck as though you were stabbing the animal as close to the backbone as possible. Cut outwards and as you go you will have cut both jugular veins and the windpipe. The animal will be dead within 30 seconds, but will have felt no pain at all.

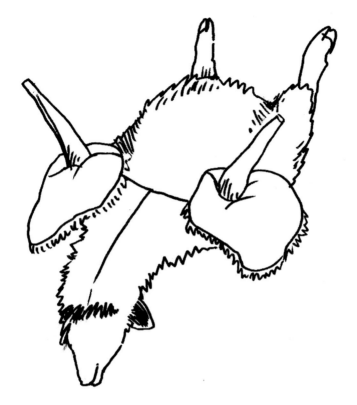

Cut the forelegs out

Some people undertake the process on straw so that the blood doesn't go everywhere and some choose to raise the animal so that the blood does not fall onto the hide.

Chop off the front feet at the bottom joint and wash your hands. From inside, cut the skin outwards with the blade outermost so that you do not cut into the meat and slit down the leg to the centre of the chest. Do this for both front legs then wash your

Cut the rear legs out

hands. Cut off the head at the highest point you can and then wash your hands again.

Remove the head from the working site so that you do not fall over it. Personally, I don't like looking at it. You can certainly cut out the tongue, which is good meat either for yourself, or for the dog.

Chop off the back hooves at the lowest joint, pull or cut away the skin from the lower leg and raise the animal on a gimbrel which is a little like a coat hanger for both legs, but you can use two chains or a good rope affair just as effectively. The gimbrel is better behind the tendon. Cut along the inside of each back leg to the back part of the anus. You might wish to wash the rear end before you do this.

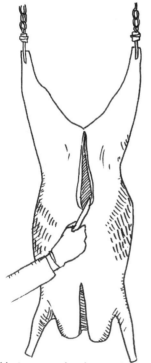

Having sawn the chest cavity but round the anus and through the belly

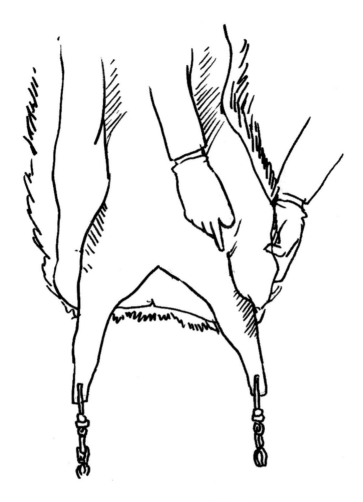

Pull away the skin with a fist - a process called fisting

Removing the skin

The removal of the skin is largely done by pushing you wet fist under the skin so that it comes away from the membrane that holds it to the rest of the body. You will need to wash your hands regularly

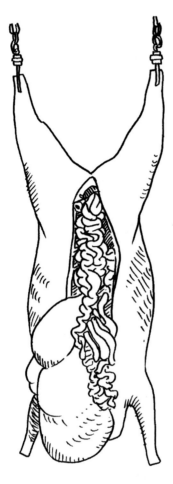

Be prepared for a lot of rumen and intestines to fall

and do keep them wet but avoid using soap.

Cut outwards with the knife uppermost from the centre of the chest where you cut earlier, along the centre of the belly and around the anus. You should now be able to remove the skin like a pullover.

The guts (not yours)

Congratulations! Where once you had a sheep, you now have food. You have done you and your family a great service. They will not starve!

Find the colon and work your hand towards the anus, pulling it out if necessary, and as near to the anus as possible. Tie this off with a piece of string to secure its contents. You will need a good bath on the floor to collect the guts.

There are lots of ways to tackle the next phase. You can saw through the breast bone and tie off the gullet at the top of the animal. Or you can find the stomach and tie it off at the top (the lower end of the gullet).

Having cut into the bone, you will hear air rushing in and you can use your fingers to gain yourself more room. Do not cut the contents of the chest.

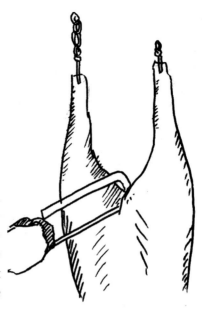

Divide the animal in half as for beef

Cutting beyond the ties, the guts should pull out easily and into your bath. You can use the intestines as sausage skins by emptying the contents, scraping away with the back of a knife and treating them with lots of water and salt, but it isn't worth it because you can buy them from suppliers packed in salt and they will last for ever (well nearly).

Now wash your hands for the thousandth time.

The bladder will be held in position by the urethra and it should be removed carefully.

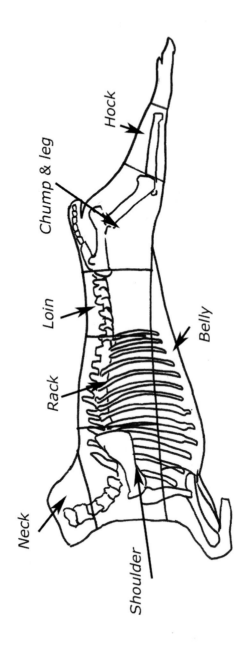

Keep the kidneys and the liver in scrupulously clean receptacles.

The pluck (heart and lungs) can be removed from the chest cavity and used, if you require. I personally don't like them, but the dog does! If you want to use the heart, cut it open to remove the clotted blood, which will begin to stink.

Wash the carcass both inside and out and hang it overnight before you cut it into joints. I cover it in a plastic sheet to keep it moist. You must avoid freezing the meat at this point.

Butchering lamb

The carcass will weigh around 20 to 25 kilos and is basically divided into three sections. The legs and chump, the middle and the neck.

Legs and chump

Find the top of the hip and make a cut straight down with the large knife. This will probably push right through the backbone, but you can use a saw if you like.

The legs should be separated by first finding the pubic bone at the front of the hips. This is easily cut through in the centre line because it is made of cartilage. The boning knife should be more than adequate for this purpose.

On the other side, cut around the sacral joints, lifting up the meat (which is actually the lower end of the fillet) and follow the bone all the way round, cutting through the cartilage of the hip joint. The leg should now fall free.

The top three inches is the chump, which should be cut off square. The aitchbone should be cut out of the leg and the extra fat and gristle cut away. Trim off the bone at the bottom, sawing through near to the knuckle and then trim away the Achilles tendon. Bone out the chump and either tie it up, cut it up as steaks, or dice it for a curry!

The middle (also known as the saddle)

This is separated from the shoulders by cutting between the sixth and seventh ribs. You probably will need to use the saw to cut through the backbone.

The middle looks like a ribcage with a backbone. Draw a line with the knife half way across the ribs, parallel to the backbone, and cut through on either side.

Now clean the fat and the other material off the backbone and anything else that looks gruesome. You will need to remove the nervous tissue from the backbone as a precaution from scrapie, the sheep form of BSE. This piece of saddle is now called the loin.

The neck end should contain the sacrum, or blade,

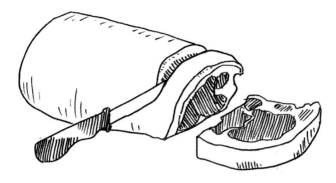

Cutting cutlets and chops

which should be cut out. You simply cut down between each rib to make lamb cutlets, and when you have run out of ribs you do the same to get lumber chops.

The flank can be boned, rolled and tied, or chopped up for mince.

Neck

Remove the scrag, which is the bit of neck sticking out of the thorax, with a knife and a saw. This can then be boned out.

Shoulder

You can do two things here. You can either saw through the backbone to give you two huge pieces of meat for further processing, or you can pare away at the flesh. I prefer to cut through the backbone, and then pare away at all the flesh from the bones around the joints and remove the shank.

This can be cut into two halves so that you can then roll up two joints per shoulder.

Notes on killing goats

A BBC news report highlighted a case where neighbours called the police after seeing blood gush from under the front door of a Northern Ireland home. The police discovered the head and entrails of a goat in the garden and the rest of the meat cooking in various pots. A second goat, an old Billy, stood in the pantry, presumably awaiting the same fate. The Ulster RSPCA took the goat and the police spoke to the occupiers, people recently arrived from Africa, 'because it might be a health and safety matter.' What is interesting to me is not that the police didn't know the law about animal slaughter, but that the people were able to buy two goats in the first place!

You can treat a goat in exactly the same way as a sheep, except that the stunning position is just beneath the ridge that extends from the base of the horn. The other proviso is that the amount of cleanliness you had for a sheep must be increased tenfold for a goat. The meat is very easily tainted, and let's be honest, it smells bad enough as it is! (My opinion – please don't write in!)

You will need plenty of water and do be especially

careful with the gut contents.

Some people simply cut away at the meat of the carcass without butchering and freeze the whole amount, diced and ready for stews and curries.

It is a point worth mentioning that the skin comes away much more easily tahn from a sheep.

Notes on butchering goats

A goat is almost identical to a lamb, although a little smaller and much more strongly flavoured. You can treat it just like a lamb if you wish. Alternatively, and this happens a lot, you can simply quarter the animal to make it easier to handle and then pare off all the meat, working methodically all around the carcass, not worrying about the joints as such, but cubing the meat for curries and stews. The fat, in particular, has a strong flavour and is somehow stringy, so make sure you are completely methodical about trimming the meat, and try, if you can, to remove every last piece of fat, gristle and connective tissue. This will help you to get a good, mild meat.

When butchering a goat, wash your hands a lot. It does tend to taint very easily and taints any other meat easily too, so be scrupulously clean.

Store goat meat separately from any other meat, in vacuum packs if possible and only freeze it well protected in plastic. If you have diced your meat, this is easy to store, but use food quality bags if you can because otherwise the meat will pick up plastic flavours.

Chapter Seven
Poultry

Rember that there are only two completely legal and economic ways to kill an animal: with a free bullet followed by bleeding or by stunning followed by bleeding but forget economics; you are not in this to make money. You will never be able to grow a chicken, kill it, prepare it and then sell it for a couple of pounds! You are in this for a better flavour, improved animal welfare, independence from the system, the use of the whole animal and a lifestyle way beyond that afforded you by buying a chicken that is labelled as 'extra tasty' on the shelves of a supermarket.

Most poultry is very easily spooked, and I believe that when they get nervous, the quality of the meat suffers. Some commentators put it down to adrenaline, but I am not sure about this personally because lot of adrenaline is pumped into the animal in the killing process, whether the animal is stunned or not.

Setting the record straight

People kill chickens all the time, by all sorts of methods but there are only two completely safe and 100% legal ways of doing it. A free bullet (a high powered airgun pellet will do) into the brain from a close distance followed by immediate bleeding, or electrical (or percussive) stunning followed again by immediate bleeding.

Why is dislocation not recommended?

You have to be very skilled to be able to ensure that the job breaks the spinal chord completely and thus kills the bird. Also, the time taken for the animal to actually die is often longer than a couple of minutes, and many have started to be plucked while still alive. For this reason, Compassion in World Farming does not believe the procedure should be recommended. The law, however, does say that poultry can be killed by neck dislocation, and we shall outline this later. We do, however, advise that such animals should be bled after the initial signs of death have taken place.

It might be argued, and may well be in law at some point, that a time of two minutes for a beast to die represents an unacceptable period, and the duty of ensuring the animal does not suffer distress or pain has been broken, thus causing an offence by law.

Similarly, all those tools used to do the same job as dislocation can cause various forms of discomfort, from mild to severe pain, and the factors which determine whether it has been a good kill or a bad kill are not always in the hands of the user.

Why is using an axe is not recommended?
You cannot be sure that in all cases a single stroke will sever the neck, and death might require a further blow, or even a third strike! Most of the equipment required to cut the throat of the bird has to be sharp by definition, but you do not always get axes which are sufficiently sharp for the job.

A bird with a damaged neck can take a surprisingly long time to die, although it has to be said that death from the severing of the head can appear to be instant, but it may take as long as 30 seconds for the bird's brain inside the head to die from a lack of blood.

The alternative

Anyone who keeps poultry for their own food is doing bird-kind a good service. Don't go telling me that you can, in any way, compare a few seconds of shocking discomfort to goodness knows how long spent in shocking discomfort in a cage or, worse still, in a broiler shed!

The instructions for one model of stunner/killer says:

"Chickens and turkeys that are unable to walk can be despatched where they lie, providing that the tool can be positioned accurately on the bird's head. Birds that are more active need to be caught and restrained, preferably in a bleeding cone, or shackled."

Dispatched where they lie means just that – the animal is in such a condition that they cannot actually move. How can any amount of humane treatment make up for a lifestyle that has created such a creature? So, in keeping with the lavish care you have given to your stock during its life, just be sure that its death is the same, whether you choose to dislocate the neck, stun and bleed or shoot and bleed.

Before killing

Handle your birds regularly so that they are not surprised when you pick them up and hold their legs. Separate the animal from other birds and deny it food for 24 hours, but do give it free access to water.

How to kill by dislocation

Collect your chicken gently and calmly and hold both legs in a firm grip with one hand. The head should be held in the other, between the middle fingers and facing outwards so the back of the head rests in the palm of the hand. Push down on the head end and twist. You will feel the bones break and the animal will begin to flap violently. Within 30 seconds the flapping will stop and the bird will be dead.

Hold or hang the bird upside down so that the blood fills the void in the neck, or cut through the neck to allow the blood to escape.

The same method is used for killing ducks, only you have to work harder because the animal is a good deal stronger. Geese should be killed by stunning and bleeding, unless you are an all-in-wrestler or a prop forward!

How to kill by bleeding

The stun
You must use a stunning method that is seen to work properly. Take it as read that the free bullet is only another way of stunning the bird. The use of a stunning hammer is of little use on poultry, leaving only an electrical stun or a percussive stun gun.

You can buy hand held electrical stunning equipment or percussion stunning equipment. We will not include detailed information on how to use this equipment as there are more than one model and design, and there is no generic mode of operation that covers everything on the market. Consequently, you will have to read the instructions on the model you use and be sure that you can use the equipment properly.

Normally, the bolt of a percussive stunner is matched to the type of bird, and you will need to make sure that you use the correct charge for the beast. NB: A poultry stunner is not guaranteed to work on a larger animal, so be sure what you are buying, and use the right equipment for the job.

Bleeding of the animal should take place within a few seconds of the stun, and the whole operation should be swift.

Use of a killing cone

The bird is inverted into the cone which allows the head to peep out at the bottom. The stunner is applied to the top of the head and fired. The cone restricts the flapping of the bird in its death convulsions, and immediately the neck is cut with a sharp blade, ensuring that both carotid arteries are cut. A firm cut round the whole underside of the neck will achieve this.

Restraint without a killing cone

You may need a partner to make sure the animal is still, and here there is danger to the humans as well as the bird. I have sometimes used a guard to hold the bird's head, allowing access for the stunner. This guard is a simple home made device created from three pieces of wood which simply holds the head still, with someon else holding the body of the bird.

I have found the methods where you insert a sharp knife into the brain or down the throat to cut the arteries to be too cumbersome for my fat fingers. Some American publications describe a process whereby the bird is held upside down until 'it falls asleep' and is then stuck into the brain with a sharp knife. This is certainly not allowed in the UK.

It is a good idea to put a bowl under the bird to catch the blood. I like to kill away from the other hens but not because it seems to upset them. In fact they seem to have an innate tendency towards cannibalism, and they will actually fight over spilled chicken blood.

Is it dead?

The bird is dead when the convulsions cease and the eyes close. A good stun, particularly a percussive stun, usually kills the animal outright, and it will convulse. If the bird continues to breathe rhythmically it is stunned, but there is no time to wait to inspect it. If you miss-stun you will certainly know about it, and so will the bird. You should then kill the animal right away by neck dislocation.

Once stunned properly, get in there and slit its throat. Only then should you start to pluck. You should wait two minutes before starting to pluck the feathers, which you should do with sharp pulls against the grain, starting with the flight feathers.

Some people dip the bird in hot water at around 60°C for a minute and pluck it wet. This can certainly help, especially with bigger birds.

Dressing

It's a bit odd calling this dressing as it is more like an extreme form of undressing!

First cut under the skin at the base of the neck bone and continue to cut up towards the head. Then remove the head by cutting the bones. Open up the skin around the neck and chop off the feet near to the 'knee'.

At the other end, cut around the anus, or vent, taking care to avoid cutting through the guts. When it is fully cut out, pull away at the skin, so that you have a hole. Then cut the skin from the hole you have just created to the breastbone. You now have

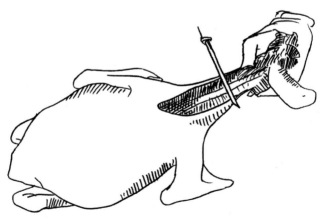

Pull the head and remove it as close to the body as you can

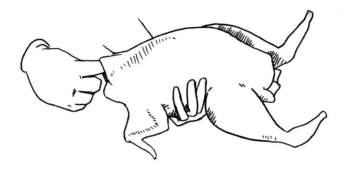

Pull out the neck and crop if you can reach

Having cut round the vent and up to the breast bone, get your hands in
and pull everything out

a hand-sized hole.

Place the bird it on some newspaper and get your
fingers inside, or even your whole hand, and draw
out the whole of the insides. You should find this
will include the liver, heart and lungs.

Now wash the bird thoroughly both inside and out
under plenty of running water.

You can keep both the liver and heart if you want
and use them either to make gravy or to feed the

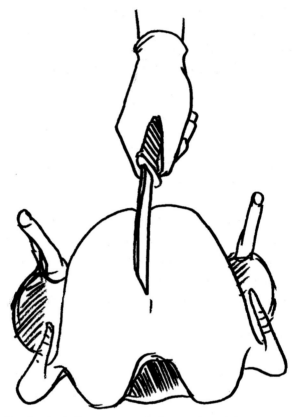

Slice with a boning knife to remove the breasts if needed

dog.

Back at the head end, pull out the neck bones and the crop. You can use the neck bones to make an excellent stock. Similarly, when you have cooked the bird and removed the meat, you can also boil the bones (with their associated bits of skin and meat) and make yet more stock or a delicious soup.
Exactly the same process is used for turkeys, ducks and geese, only it's a little bit messier. Actually, I

find larger birds easier to deal with because I can get my meat plates of hands inside them more easily. It is worth repeating that you might find it easier to dunk a large bird to ease the plucking.

Hanging

This is a matter of personal taste. Some people do hang poultry, such as pheasant. Personally, I'm not that keen; if I wanted to eat cooked, putrefying bacteria, I'd go for a take away. The idea is that bacteria increase the pH of the meat and thus make it more tender. I certainly wouldn't want to hang a bird for more than three days, although I know that some of you will throw your hands up in disgust and say this is nothing like long enough.

The big clean

Even if you have treated your hens against all manner of diseases, the whole of the workspace, your tools and you too will need to be disinfected. Any animal waste will need to be incinerated and certainly not fed to anything. (I know I can't resist giving things to the dog and he can't resist eating them but, since we are not planning to eat the dog, I don't suppose it really matters).

Chicken choppings

The best way to do this, in my opinion, is to roast the chicken whole, and then keep the carcass for making soup. However, you can fillet the chicken, if you like.

Place your bird breast up and from the top of the breastbone, cut close to the bone with a small boning knife. Take this cut down as far as the wishbone, and pare away at the whole muscle, which will eventually fall away into your hand.

To remove the skin, get hold of the corner and push your knife in between the flap and the muscle. Pull at the skin to remove it.

Now hold up the wing and push it back. It will pop out of its joint, and should be cut out there.

Do the same with the leg to push it out of its socket. Cut at the joint that is now broken and, with a small knife, take all the muscle off the leg. You can remove the skin in the same way. (I personally like the skin, so I choose to keep it on. It is the tastiest but possibly the most fattening bit of the bird!)

There really is a lot more meat on the bird, but it ican be difficult to get off, so I simply boil the lot for stock and then pick away at the meat. The olives in the hip are gorgeous! I normally get enough meat off the remaining carcass for four chicken sandwiches! Heaven!

The best tip!

The first time I dressed an animal – it was actually a rabbit – I couldn't eat for a few days; I had become so accustomed to supermarket sourced meat. So I came up with the plan of dressing a number of birds (or any animal) on the same day, putting them in the freezer and going away to eat grass and apples for a few days, after which time I am more than ready for a good roast chicken!

Chapter Eight
Pigeon and Humble pie

If you can shoot a pigeon with a gun, you are certainly a better man than me. My cartridge to kill ratio is somewhere in the high twenties, and at that rate pigeon meat costs me a fortune. Once shot, the animal should have its neck dislocated in the usual way, just in case it isn't properly dead, though with experience you will know exactly which animals need this. The important thing is to be calm and avoid excitement. I myself was once nearly shot by an idiot who decided he had to shoot a bird a second time!

Needless to say that the only pigeons to shoot are country ones. I really wouldn't fancy eating the ones that hang around railway bridges or spend their days depositing droppings on dubious Victorian statues in most of our city centres.

A lot of people simply remove the breasts, these being the only real source of meat on the bird. Pluck the feathers on the breast and slice down the breastbone. You can get your fingers inside the skin and around the muscle, which can then be easily cut out with a sharp knife.

While you are at it you might want to cut open the crop. You will see what the animal has been eating, and you will find it packed full of corn or cabbage or some other valuable crop, and when you multiply this by a few hundred in that locality you will see how important it is that this animal should be kept under control.

Pigeons are easily dressed (or drawn, whichever word you prefer) in the same way as a chicken, it is just a more delicate process. Keep the liver, which can be fried or ground to a paste and made into a great stuffing or a rich pate.

Other game birds

Oh! Such a lot of rubbish (in my opinion) is spoken about game birds. Firstly, I agree with the late lamented Jack Hargreaves, who abhorred the

Pull the feathers from the breast

Continental Battue introduced by the Victorians, where the country estate becomes a mini version of the Somme as hundreds of birds are filed past a set of rich folk to run the gauntlet of shot. The Old English way was always the rough shoot, where a brace of birds for the pot was all that was needed and the fun was in working with the dogs, not in hobnobbing with the rich folk.

Anyway, it is really easy to spoil a game bird, pheasant, partridge or anything. Don't pile them up if you have more than one, and don't put them in the boot. The thing to do is get the heat out of them as soon as you can, and this means getting their insides out there and then, if at all possible.

First, make sure the animal is dead. Then pluck all the breast feathers in a line from the breastbone to the anus and make a cut (you can use sharp scissors, or a really sharp knife with the point facing upwards) down to and round the anus. The insides will pull out easily and you should be able to pull the lungs and crop out through the same hole. Some people then pack the cavity with grass to soak up the blood.

Plucking should be done as soon as possible, the underside first and then the back. Singe off the tiny, downy feathers with a blowtorch. You will need to wash out the inside and outside of the bird, remove

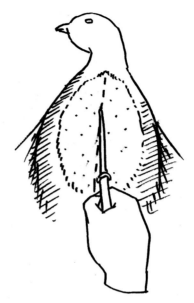

Cut out the breast meat with the boning knife

the remnants of organs you didn't manage in the field and then freeze it. I prefer to remove the head and feet, pull out the neck bones like a chicken and place it inside a plastic bag for freezing. I do not hang the birds in any way.

Chapter Nine
Rabbits and Squirrel

In France, and to a lesser extent in the UK, people farm rabbits. There are a number of companies whose aim is to collect live animals from strategic points and transport these on for slaughter. These are caged animals that are processed centrally. The home bred animal is a much more robust beast than the wild rabbit and there is really only one means of killing available and that is to stun and bleed. In the case of the rabbit, electrical stunning is used because butchers still like to display the animal with an unblemished head.

It is unusual for people to keep, kill and eat rabbits that have been kept privately. It is a shame we do not eat so much rabbit in this country, especially when you realise that it is one of the best meats you can eat and very low in both fat and cholesterol.

There are really only two ways of killing a rabbit. One of those methods is with a free bullet (preferably a .22 from a rifle) although the most powerful airguns will do a good job as long as you have a head shot. Shooting the animal is within the law and is specified as being 'in the field'. This doesn't literally have to be in a field, but should be in a position where the bullet will exit only into soil, without injuring any other animal or person. The animal's neck should be sliced through as soon as possible, within less than a few seconds, if possible.

Animals caught by the common use of mist netting, using ferrets, can still be killed by neck dislocation. It is important that the dogs are trained only to drive the rabbits into nets, and not to attack them. This would be illegal under the hunting with dogs legislation.

Killing a rabbit by neck dislocation

The back legs are held in one hand and the head cupped in the other, in a backwards position so that the fingers are near the ears. Holding tightly, the animal is stretched by pulling with both hands until the neck breaks. This is exactly the same as for a chicken. The knee can be used if the length of the rabbit makes it difficult for the killer to easily extend the arm. The animal is then stretched over the knee, achieving the same result. The rabbit should then be bled immediately by severing the neck.

On farm killing of rabbits should be done by electrical stunning and slicing the neck as soon as possible afterwards.

The usual American method of killing rabbits involves holding the animal by the back legs and hitting it sharply on the back of the head with a heavy club. It is difficult to know if this is allowed under UK law, but might be if the animal is subsequently bled by cutting its neck.

In all case, the target animal should be checked to ensure it is dead before moving on to the next stage. The death of shot animals should always be confirmed by an:

- Absence of rhythmic, respiratory movements
- Absence of eye protection reflex (corneal reflex) or 'blink'
- A fixed, glazed expression in the eyes
- Loss of colour in mucous membranes (becoming mottled and pale without refill after pressure is applied)

If you are lamping (shining a lamp into a rabbit's eyes at night so they freeze before shooting them), you must observe strict discipline to avoid injury to each other. Only shoot a certain number of animals, each time firing in the same direction and being in no doubt of the land beyond the shot.

Make a nick in the belly with a sharp knife

As quickly as possible after shooting, once all the guns are confirmed as safe and out of use, each animal should be checked to ensure it is dead.

Killing squirrels

These are becoming ever more popular for eating, and should be treated as rabbits, except that I defy anyone to catch one in order to kill it by stunning or bleeding. It should be noted that

Pull the rip down the belly with your fingers

only grey squirrels should be taken, and you would do well only to take squirrels from a completely rural situation.

Dressing, drawing and paunching both rabbits and squirrels

It is not mentioned much in the literature, but rabbits should be 'peed,' once killed, to avoid strongly smelling urine spoiling the meat. This is done by firm pressure on either side of the midline of the lower abdomen using the thumbs.

If the weather is warm the animal should be eviscerated straight away to remove the heat.

Rabbits are traditionally carried in the following manner. The skin between the Achilles tendon is split and the opposite leg is pushed through the hole to create a loop that allows the animal to be carried on a pole, along with several of his friends. There are a number of ways of dealing with a rabbit. You can chop off its head and paws. You can then slit the belly skin from the breastbone to the anus, which is cut around to free the entrails. You need to keep the knife point uppermost. The slit can easily be torn open using your fingers.

Next reach inside and draw out the intestines onto newspaper and, using a broad knife or your fingers, pull out the lungs, heart and liver, being careful with the gall bladder. Now cut off the tail and pull the legs out of the skin, which should be pulled with a minimum of effort. Draw the skin back until it falls off the carcass.

Another method is to remove the paws, save for one

back one. Then hook the animal over the hock and make a slit in the groin, through which you can pull the legs.

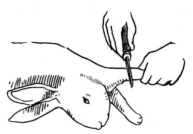

Remove the feet

Cut round the anus and remove the tail and, at this point, draw out the intestines. Now reach inside and remove the rest of the innards. You can then pull the skin down until it is loose everywhere and remove the animal from the hook. Finally, cut off the remaining paw.

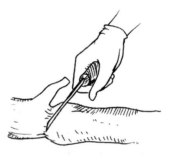

Pull the skin over the body and head and then remove the head while covered in skin

Pull the skin back and remove the head with the skin covering it and wash the carcass inside and out. Now you can quarter it and this is best done using a cleaver. You should end up with two shoulders, two back segments, two loin segments and two legs.

Treat squirrels in precisely the same manner, except that it will only provide two shoulders and two legs.

Chapter Ten
Seafood and Fish

I personally think fish get a very raw deal. I have heard of anglers who will rip the face off a fish in order to remove their hook, and then leave it with blood running from its gills in the alien environment (to the fish, not us!) of the open air. And yes, before you write in, I do know that people do not farm fish in the general smallholding sense, but there are a considerable number of people who rely on a catch to supplement their protein as part of their self-sufficiency regime.

A smallholder would be short-sighted to ignore the fact that the UK is surrounded by some of the best seafood in the world! There is everything from limpets to lobsters to be found and enjoyed. Indeed, a day's outing to the seaside can provide a veritable feast of fantastic food, but what we say about killing a pig must surely apply to killing a shrimp. If you are humane with animals that have bright eyes and look at you in a cuddly and forlorn manner, then you have to be exactly the same with any animal, even if it has lots of legs, or indeed no legs at all!

Killing crustaceans

Crustaceans refers to shrimp, prawns, langoustines, crabs, crayfish and lobsters (and even woodlice!).

I am writing this chapter on Anglesey and just around the corner from me is a garden with about a hundred lobster creels whose owner goes out to get lobster to sell illegally. This doesn't mean you cannot catch your own for your kitchen, but simply implies that you cannot sell your catch.

Ideally. all large crustaceans (crabs and lobsters mostly) should be chilled before killing them in boiling water. They do suffer stress when out of the water, and there is evidence of a high degree of sentience, particularly in lobsters; they are capable of thought and do make decisions. The chilling process, which should be done in a freezer for around four hours, turns off their central nervous system. When they are then placed into the boiling water they will feel no pain and will be dead within a matter of seconds.

Shrimps and prawns should be killed by immersion in a large quantity of boiling water on a large fire or burner, so that when they are tossed alive into the pot their own body temperature does not cause the water to go below the boiling point. You need to ensure that the final animal goes into the water at the same temperature as the first. The main thing is to ensure that they are killed on the beach if possible, or better still, on the boat! Certainly a mass of shrimps caught with a shrimping net should be killed and cooked there and then but can be cleaned and potted back at home.

Try to pour them in in small handfuls so that there

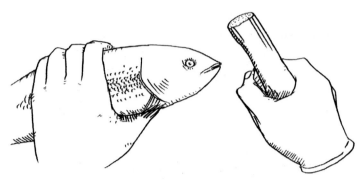

Kill the fish straight away with a sharp blow to the top of the head

is no chance of any localised cooling of the water below the boilingin the pot. These animals will be dead within half a second and should be cooked in around a minute. I am not going to discuss killing molluscs, which should be treated rather like crustaceans, at least in the case of the bigger ones, snails (before you ask, no! I haven't) and cuttlefish, if you're lucky enough to find them. And I know nothing of the well known biting technique while the octopus is trying to push its tentacles down your throat and biting you with its beak!

Under no circumstances should you ever put them in a pan of cold water and then bring it to the boil.

Killing fish

Please, please, please kill your fish before you remove the hook. I know I am courting controversy here, and some of my friends are among the most famous fishermen in the land, but I can only think of two reasons for dragging a fish out of the water on a hook. The first reason is to practice. We need fishing skills. They are important and if you believe that it is right to eat animals, then it is certainly right to eat fish, but these skills only come with practice. The other reason for fishing is to eat.

Slit on the belly cutting too dep as far as the vent, remove the head and clean out the inside

Once the animal is out of the water, hit it with a Priest (a heavy stick designed for the purpose) on the flat of the head. Repeat the stroke as hard as you can very quickly after the first and the animal will

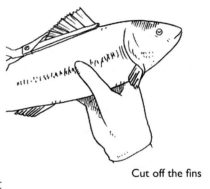

Cut off the fins

be dead. The brain is quite near the surface at the top of the head, between the eyes.

Then you can remove your hook! If you can manage it, dead fish should be gutted as soon as possible and stored in cold water, ice or, in the case of herring, salt.

Cleaning

Of course, if you were to ask it, the fish would have protested that it was already clean. Use a reasonably sharp knife and stroke the skin from the tail to the head to remove the scales.

Use a sharp knife to make a shallow slit from the vent at the bottom to the gills at the top. Cut off the head and scrape out the entrails onto a newspaper. Use a pair of scissors to remove the fins all over the body. Then wash it under running water and pat it dry on a kitchen towel.

Filleting

Use a sharp knife and cut a slit along the back to the backbone.

Pare away at the flesh by the bones in long and firmly controlled strokes, so that the whole comes away as a single piece. Use tweezers to pull out any remaining bones.

Trout should be cooked with the bones in place since the meat is easily lifted off once the fish is sliced. Salmon can be cut transversley as steaks.

Chapter Eleven
Waste Not, Want Not

In this book there has been a lot of talk about the nobility of the farm animal and how, having given its life for our dinner, we should not waste any of it. In today's 'throwaway' culture, we have a psychological problem. We throw away what we no longer want or can't use, but we also throw away what we do not want to see or cannot stomach. We only want palatable, easy to eat, easy on the eye food that does not resemble the real, biologically messy material it came from. Consequently, we have fish fingers, beef burgers, chicken nuggets, cheese straws, crab sticks, cheese triangles and turkey twizzlers. All of them are universally bad, filled with cheap meat. 'Lips and backsides,' my grandfather would have said, 'like a cheap sausage.' And all these items of 'food' bear absolutely no resemblance to their source animal

Now, there is nothing wrong with eating 'lips and backsides' if you know that that is what you are eating, but it amazes me that people will not eat some of the basic dishes which were so common just a generationor so ago.

Tanning

Making a sheepskin

If you simply leave your skins, they will rot like any other natural material, becoming stiff and smelling very bad in the process. You can easily cure your sheepskins if you use the right materials and are prepared to spend a little time. In the past, this was done with mixtures of urine, water, saltpetre and salt. The use of potash alum has made the process simpler and slightly more palatable.

Firstly, wash your sheepskin in cold water in a bath. Any blood on the wool can be sprinkled with salt and the process should take a day with several changes of water.

A good wash to remove the grit and oils

Give the fleece a good wash with some mild soap flakes (not biological ones, nor washing up liquid) and rinse it completely to remove the soap and grime.

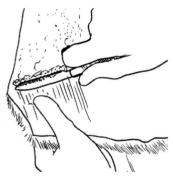

Scraping the inside gunk away

The inside of the skin is then scraped to remove the lanolin, flesh, fat and 'bits' from the

Soaking the skin with curing salts

inside and the fleece soaked for three days in a curing solution. There are several recipes for this.

To 5 litres of water you need to add 250g of potash alum, 250g of salt and a teaspoon of saltpetre. You will need about 25 litres of this mixture in total.

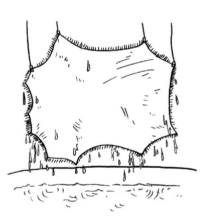

Alow the skin to drip dry

When this is over, allow the fleece to drip dry over the bath you soaked it in (NOT your own domestic bath by the way!) until it stops dripping.

You can then stretch the skin by nailing it to a board, fur down, leaving the skin outermost. Then you rub neatsfoot oil thoroughly into the skin a couple of times over a couple of days, after which it should be allowed to dry. It is worth noting that some people mix the neatsfoot oil with soap flakes dissolved in a cup of water to make it easier to use.

Now for the hard bit. You will have to work the skin

Peg out and braining the skin

hard over a chair, skin side down. The skin will be really stiff and the molecules have to be worked to make them subtle. The whole skin must be rubbed and you will ache, but it will be really worth it.

Other tanning

Braining

This is not a book about tanning but it is something that can be done to all skins. You can even send your skins away to be tanned for very little expense. Companies licensed to use the complex and rather poisonous chemistry do also undertake organic tanning. You can also tan at home.

Working the skin on the chair

Firstly, the skin is scraped inside to remove the fat and any other membranes. This process takes a while and should be done carefully so as not to split the skin. Then the skin is washed with soap flakes and dried.

Traditionally, a brain, which is mostly fat, is blended with a little water and rubbed well into the skin. When the skin is completely covered and worked. it is allowed to dry. The flesh is preserved by cold smoking.

An alternative is to use a combination of egg yolks and cooking oils rubbed into the skin in the same way. You can also preserve the skin by using a mixture of salt and saltpetre.

Either way you then have to work the skin in order to make it pliable. This is best done over a stretched rope or the back of a chair. Once completed, the process will give you a great skin that can be made into almost anything. It will be pliant and will allow your skin to breathe if you use it to make clothes.

Tripe

Tripe is the prepared stomach of cattle and occasionally sheep, goats or pigs. In beef tripe, the rumen, the reticulum (honeycomb), and the omasum (the first three stomachs) are used. They are slit open and washed at around 60°C in a solution of washing soda. After this, the dark layer is scraped away from the inside, leaving a creamy mass. The reticulum is the favourite because it is honeycomb and therefore holds more vinegar when served with salt, pepper and sliced tomatoes.
After the scrapings it is washed again for 15 minutes in many changes of water, then brought up to 80°C for 20 minutes. It is allowed to cool and served.

The process is the same for pigs, sheep and goats.

Brains

These are cooled, peeled, thinly sliced and are sometimes dipped in batter and fried. They are high in both fat and cholesterol. These days it is not advisable to eat brains because of a number of diseases including CJD. It is also an offence, for this reason, to allow the nervous tissue of cattle to enter into the human food chain.

Tongue

This can still be bought, jellied and cured, on the cold meat counter of some shops, but it is becoming less popular, viz our desire to eat nothing but unnatural food. (To be honest, I personally do not like the flavour).

An ox tongue is a huge piece of meat, as is a pig's tongue. It should be boiled, peeled and then cured in a strong brine solution for up to a week, after which it can be drained, washed and served.

Belly bread or pancreas

This organ is dissected out of the liver and intestines and soaked in water for 30 minutes with a little salt, then left to drain. The ducts and any other vessels are trimmed, along with the fat, and fried, and traditionally served with eggs and bacon.

Ribs

Pork ribs come as a surprise to people used to 'spare ribs' from the take away. A full sheet is chopped in half and cured for two days in a spiced bacon cure. They are then boiled and served with potatoes and cabbage. The sheet is divided into portion sized pieces and the eater pulls the bones apart with the fingers to get to the meat. It is a true finger picker's delight!

Marrow

Bone marrow was widely used in cooking and you can still get dishes which use this ingredient in some restaurants. Victorian marrow spoons are no longer made, but they should be. You can pull out the marrow whole by cracking the bone open with a cleaver and add it to gravy. Some people toast it with a little salt, on bread.

Fat

These days people simply cut out the fat from their meat and throw it away. When you have your own animal butchered there is often a huge amount of fat that can be used for all sorts of processes, from cooking to lubrication and even lighting.

Place your fat into a large stainless steel pot that has a lid. You don't need the lid but keep it handy just incase it catches fire, which is a rare event and hasn't happened to me (as yet). If it does, simply turn off the heat, place the lid in position and throw a wet towel over the lid. The fire will go out and you should let the pan cool down.

To render, simply put the fat on a low heat and continuously stir and scrape it around the pan. As the fat melts, carefully ladle it into warm pots, allowing them to cool and the fat to set. They can be frozen to keep the fat fresh. This process works well with tallow, which is beef and sheep fat, and lard, which is pig fat.

Another method is to put the fat into a large container of boiling water. Boil away for 30 minutes and then strain. The liquid can then be poured into a large dish and cooled. The fat will rise to the surface and cake. This can then be spooned away.

Gelatine

Clean your pig's feet, scraping away any of the dirt and debris you find, until all you have is perfectly clean skin. Place them in a pan three quarters full of water and boil. Reduce the liquid by half by allowing it to simmer, a process which should take at least an hour, and then add a little more water every now and again and simmer away until the feel fall apart in the pan and you are left with what looks like an alien. Use a spoon to remove any scum during the process.

Finally, strain the liquid into a bowl and cool it slowly. You will have the very best jelly for your pies and anything else you might need.

Sausage skins

We have already mentioned in this book that you can buy specially cleaned and salted sausage skins. These are by far the best ones to use, but in the spirit of self-sufficiency you can make your own. Of course you can use beef, pig or sheep casings and these will easily produce enough skins for the sausages you need to make from that particular animal, as well as stomach for haggis and other products.

Pull the intestines apart and force their contents out. Wash both inside and out and then use a piece of appropriately sized dowel to turn the skins inside out. This is a slippery procedure. I have done it by tying a knot at around 30 cm from one end and then pushing the loose end onto the dowel. Push the stick with the intestine into itself so that by the time you have gone past the knot you are slipping the thing inside out.

This is then carefully scraped all around with a knife and the whole thing soaked in brine. To get the right strength of brine you can do the egg test. This involves using an un-boiled egg which will usually sink but, as you add salt to the water, the egg will eventually float. As soon as the egg floats your concentration of water and salt is just right!

After a couple of days the whole lot is washed and the end of the skin tied to a plastic or wooden ring and packed in salt until it is to be used.

Blood

It is unfortunate that all the black puddings in this country are made from pelleted and treated blood, mostly imported from Holland. There are a lot of regulations about the use of blood in food and the collecting of a bucket of blood from your own pig does still seem to be possible, although you will not be able to collect the blood from your own pig if you send it to the abattoir. 10% salt is added to the bucket to stop it from clotting, which usually means adding a handful as the blood pours into the washed bucket. If you can, get yourself an enamelled tin bucket. This can be cleaned easily and, at the same time, transmits heat more effectively than a plastic bucket.

Black pudding is made from oats and barley used in equal quantities and twice the amount of blood. There is a lot of fat, the same amount as cereal, and spices such as mace, coriander and pepper.

The fat and cereal is cooked together for a few minutes and then the blood is added. The loose mass is put into tied casings and simmered in boiling water on a very low heat for 20 minutes. They will last a week in the fridge.

It is not a good idea to use blood as tomato feed or to compost it.

Special notes

Smell

Part of this book is an attempt to relay what it feels like to kill an animal. You can imagine that since many animals smell pretty badly on the outside, some of their insides can be pretty awful too. This can be overcome to some extent by hosing down with cold water. Many of the chemicals of the body cavity can become pretty rancid at times. A good spray with a hose with a shower attachment on the end is a good idea. Once you have cooled the animal, it does become easier to deal with in the nose department.

For this reason you might consider what can happen to cut surfaces as the blood congeals, after which it can begin to smell distinctly unpleasant. All cut surfaces are bathed in blood to a greater or lesser extent, and I tend to give the meat a quick rinse before I store or use it. Otherwise the blood will go off very quickly and it can then spoil the meat. The big factor here is the changes which can occur in domestic temperatures. It can be difficult to keep a room in a house cool and blood does go off very quickly at room temperature. It is better to store large pieces of meat rather than smaller ones, because there is comparatively less surface area for the volume of meat. (No, I am not going into the mathematics of it!)

Trimmings of meat should be used as soon as

possible and not stored. There are good reasons for this. You need to understand that many of these relate to the fact that you are doing this at home and not in controlled premises. Thin pieces of meat, with large surface areas compared to volume, can attract microbes more easily, warm up and cool down more quickly and have a greater vulnerability to spoiling than larger cuts of meat.

If you want mince or chunks of meat, use a large cut wherever possible.

But returning to the subject of smells, humans have a comparatively poor sense of smell. A dog, for example, has a sense of smell infinitely better than ours. It is not uncommon for animals to refuse to enter areas where killing has taken place, and this is usually down to the smell. For cleanliness and animal welfare purposes, make sure that the area you killed, as well as where you butchered, is cleaned completely with the appropriate disinfectant. Equipment often overlooked includes hooks, chains, tractors and fork lifts trucks. Make sure it is all washed thoroughly.

Waste

The law forbids the disposal of rotting meat in the land fill system. Nervous tissue has to be incinerated, and you are always best to do exactly the same. Your Local Authority will be able you help you with their requirements. Some have dedicated collections of waste for incineration. In some places you will have to pay but in others it is free. In some local authority areas someone will want to come and have a look at you and assess your needs.

Road Kill

The law regarding road kill is cunningly clever. You are not permitted to take animals you have accidentally killed yourself. This is designed to stop you from driving headlong into any animal that looks tasty, in order to kill it. This would clearly make you a danger to both yourself and others.

Any animal you find on the road might have been dead for ages and could be quite unsuitable for food. Do not take an animal if it is cold, or if it is the height of summer, unless you know how long it has been dead.

If it is a farm animal you are obliged to find out who owns it and if it is game you must consult the landowner. Otherwise you are in danger of being prosecuted for poaching. As you are taking it, a quick call to the police is the best course of action. By the way, if you do hit an animal it is not liable for insurance – you will have to pay out!

Finally, before you take it, make sure the animal is actually dead. It is no fun driving down the road with a once unconscious deer suddenly waking up on the back seat – believe me!

Organisations

Humane Slaughter Association

The Humane Slaughter Association was founded in 1911. It is a UK charity, concerned exclusively with promoting the humane treatment of all food animals worldwide, including cattle, sheep, pigs, poultry, fish and minority species such as deer. Their remit relates to markets, welfare of animals in and during transport, and at slaughter. It undertakes research and does a lot of training. They are more known for their work with slaughtermen and do not have a great deal to do with individuals wishing to kill their animals. They do, however, have a lot of information on killing animals – particularly on the way the law informs practice.

Dissemination of information in these areas through publications, workshops, conferences, training and consultation, is a core part of the HSA's work in seeking to achieve and continually improve best practice.

Some of their publications include:

Caring to the End, a guide to the humane dispatch of livestock for smallholders, hobby farmers and those who keep farm animals as pets.

Practical Slaughter of Poultry, a guide for the small producer, now in its 2nd edition.

Humane Killing of Livestock Using Firearms 2nd edition which gives guidance on the use of shotguns or free bullet weapons including information on correct gun operation, ballistics, how animals should be shot, types of equipment available, using the right ammunition, safety and maintenance.

Captive Bolt Stunning of Livestock 4th Edition which advises on the use of captive-bolt equipment including how it works, effective stunning, bleeding, restraint and safety.

They also produce a large number of training videos and DVD's on the subject including:

Emergency Slaughter Video
Practical Guidance on the Humane Killing of Injured, Diseased and Non-Viable Livestock.
Humane Slaughter - Taking Responsibility, a training package for all those handling and slaughtering cattle, sheep and pigs (including a video, workbook and instructor's notes).

Poultry Slaughter - Taking Responsibilit, a DVD training package for all those involved with the catching, transport and slaughter of poultry (including a DVD and a booklet).

A large number of H.S.A. publications are available on the internet and are particularly useful.

You can contact the H.S.A. at
Humane Slaughter Association

The Old School,
Brewhouse Hill,
Wheathampstead,
Herts, AL4 8AN, UK
Tel: +44 (0)1582 831919
Fax: +44 (0)1582 831414

www.hsa.org,uk
Email: info@hsa.org.uk

Compassion in World Farming (CIWF)

This is a multi-national campaigning organisation that has a remit for food animals at every stage of farming. They are more interested in lobbying governments in the humane treatment of any animals used for food. They are against cruelty, but not against the killing of animals for food. They are the group behind the continued phasing out of use of neck dislocation in chickens, the campaign against battery hens, the caging of veal calves, campaigns on pig welfare, the transport of farm animals abroad for long distances, campaigns against fur farming and many more.

They have a number of videos and booklets available, though not instructional to anyone who is interested in this field, including:

CIWF: Farm Animals & Us, an educational video about farm animal welfare for the 10-16 age group

Association for the Study of Animal Behaviour:

Stimulus Response is a video that considers the intelligence, abilities, needs and behaviour of farm animals

They also produce a series of reports:
The Global Benefits of Eating Less Meat - 2004
Reducing Meat Consumption: The Case for Urgent Reform (Summary)
Intensive Farming & the Welfare of Farmed Animals (Educational publication)
Stop - Look - Listen: Recognising the Sentience of Farm Animals (Summary)

You can contact the CIWF at
CIWF
River Court,
Mill Lane,
Godalming,
Surrey,
GU7 1EZ
Tel: +44 (0)1483 521950
www.ciwf.org.uk

The English Beef and Lamb Executive (EBLEX)

This organisation will be of use to smallholders who are looking to expand their animal output in order to sell their livestock for meat. They are the people to contact if you are considering the Quality Standard Mark for British beef and lamb.

They produce a series of beef and lamb bulletins and provide DEFRA information on diseases.

EBLEX
Graphic House
Ferrars Road
Huntingdon
Cambs
PE29 3EE
Tel: +44 (0)870 242 1394
Email: admin@eblex.org.uk

The Poultry Club of Great Britain

This association is more related to showing poultry, but there is a series of advice pages on their website that refers to the welfare of poultry. They are also of use when it comes to the conservation of rare breeds of poultry and on bio-security issues. They should be of particular interest to people worried or troubled by avian flu.

Their real value to the smallholder is perhaps the vast wealth of information their members have. A telephone call will give you the all the information you could possibly need – in fact you will probably get too much information – but all expert, all relevant and friendly.

You can contact the Poultry Club of Great Britain at:
The Poultry Club,
South Lodge,
Creeton Road,
Swinstead,
Grantham,

Lincs
NG33 4PG
Tel: 01476 550067 (Office hours are Monday to Saturday 9am-1pm)

RSPCA

These are good people who focus on the welfare of animals, as you would expect. There have been a number of incidents where people who live in urban or suburban areas have been reported to the RSPCA for cruelty by neighbours for killing poultry.

The RSPCA have guidelines for killing food animals and it will be up to you to show that your practice is better than that specified in RSPCA guidelines, which can be found at www.rspca.org.uk. Take the opportunity to show how wonderfully your animals are kept and how happy and healthy they are!

The Department for the Environment, Food and Rural Affairs (DEFRA)

The portal to the government is awash with useful information, particularly where it pertains to the law. All the directives are available in PDF format from their website, and there are in-depth guidelines relating not only to animal slaughter but to the processing of meat, the selling of meat and the registration as a food business, a must for anyone wishing to sell their own meat.

If you have access to the website, all you need to do is to put the relevant word in the search box, 'animal slaughter' for example, and all the relevant documents will appear for your use.

DEFRA is charged with the implementation of animal welfare law, as well as the protection of the public, so any important changes in the way we have to work will appear here first. Changes to the OTM scheme, for instance, will come directly from DEFRA.

You can contact DEFRA at:
Defra
Customer Contact Unit
Eastbury House
30 - 34 Albert Embankment
London
SE1 7TL
Tel: +44 (0) 20 7238 6951
www.defra.gov.uk

Meat Hygiene Service

The Meat Hygiene Service (MHS) is responsible for the protection of public health and animal health and welfare in Great Britain. They have a remit to inspect any meat, animal or facility in the UK to enforce animal welfare and public health law. It is interesting how animal welfare and public health go hand in hand.

You can get a wealth of information here from

topics such as food safety, cleanliness, hygiene, courses on food handling, packaging, presentation, microbiological contamination and chemical security. Their website is a must for anyone looking to produce their own food and is essential reading if you are thinking of going into the food business.

You are best advised to contact the Meat Hygiene Service and the Food Standards Agency on their website at www.food.gov.uk and their on line contacts section gives you every possible telephone number relating to food and food hygiene.

Supplies

Finding an abattoir

This is easier said than done for many reasons, not least that they do not advertise so readily to escape the notice of various animal rights groups. In the UK they have reduced in number tremendously and many organisations are calling for the licensing of mobile slaughtermen; an old system out of favour at the moment.

You can find a list of abattoirs near you on the internet by visiting www.sheriffratings.com/ where you can input your locality. You will be given a list, which can be fairly sparse in some parts of the country. As a word of caution, some of those included in list for my locality were not actually abattoirs, so do ask the question.

Equipment

Scobies Direct

Scobies is an online store specialising in butcher's supplies. You can buy knives, coats, hooks, mincers, mixers, ingredients, skins, gloves and even sawdust, twine and meat nets. In fact everything you need for butchering. And in certain circumstances you can get it the same day, just in case you snap your large butcher's knife inside a beef carcass.

Scobie & Junor (Estd. 1919) Ltd.
1 Singer Road
East Kilbride
Glasgow, Scotland
G75 0XS
Tel: 0800 783 7331 (free phone)
www.scobiesdirect.com

Weschenfelder

This company is dedicated to sausage making and has been making sausage skins and materials for sausages for over 80 years. The founder of the company brought his knowledge from Germany in the early years of the last century.

They specialise in making sausage kits, amongst other things, which anyone can use, from beginners to those more advanced. They also stock a range of butchering equipment.

Weschenfelder
2-4 North Road
Middlesborough
Cleveland
TS2 1DE
Tel: 01642 247524
www.weschenfelder.co.uk

Northern Tool and Equipment

These people have a great range of meat saws and an electric one that is quite cheap and within the reach of the home farmer. You might think a couple of hundred pounds is a lot to pay out, but try sawing ten sheep in half by hand!

Unit 2
Interchange Park
Portsmouth
Hampshire
PO3 5QD
0800 169 2266
www.northerntooluk.com

EasyEquip.co.uk

This company sells a fantastic range of butchers tables and blocks, as well as benches, racking and sinks. It is ideal for the dairy too.

EasyEquip.co.uk
Unit 2B
9-15 Elthorne Road
London
United Kingdom
N19 4AJ
Tel:0207 2729300

A.W.Smith & Sons

Smiths have a great website where you can actually see the products all together for easy comparison. You can spot what you need and the products are very well described.

You can get anything from the best knives and cleavers to meat thermometers and even replica meat – just to show off!

A.W.Smith & Sons (Sundries) Ltd.
The Food Trades Centre
82-88 Sherlock Street
Birmingham
B5 6LT
www.awsmith.co.uk
Tel: 0121 622 2137

Spices

Many of the companies already mentioned are also excellent sources of pre-mixed spice for sausage making.

Continental Meat Technology

www.continentalmeattechnology.co.uk
Tel: 01908 584489

You can buy skins and spice mixes and the recipes are free.

Spice World

www.spiceworld.uk.com
Tel: 02380 675777

Almost every spice you could possibly imagine.

Steenbergs

www.steenbergs.co.uk
Tel: 01765 640088

Organic spices, organic sausage blends and organic salt and pepper.

General

Ascott Smallholding Supplies

www.ascott.biz
Tel: 0845 130 6285

Here you can get absolutely anything for the smallholding, from grinders to rusk.

The Sausage Book
By Paul Peacock

Aimed at the small-scale sausage maker this book explores the development of the sausage and gives important guidance on the do's and don'ts of sausage making, tips and plenty of recipes, including age-old traditional English bangers and regional variations, as well as step-by-step guides on liniing and an excellent resource section. ISBN 978-1-904871-17-0

Venison and Garlic Sausage	
Ingredients	Method
Basic Filling 1kg Venison 500g Un-smoked fat bacon 200g Breadcrumbs or rusk 200ml Red wine	Thoroughly mix the dry ingredients so that the salt, pepper and spices are completely incorporated
Seasoning 10g Salt 10g Black pepper 10g Sugar 15g Sage 5 Crushed garlic cloves 5g Allspice 5g Marjoram	Finely grind the bacon. Coursely grind the venison Crush and finely mince the garlic Mix all the ingredients.
Casings 2 metres of hog casing, soaked for at least an hour and washed inside and out	Stuff into casings and link Leave for 24 hours to mature
Tip: You can add some Dijon mustard to the mix or some mustard powder.	

The Smoking and Curing Book
By Paul Peacock

Whether you plan to build a smoker to process your own produce or simply wish to smoke a few kippers and a little bacon in the family kitchen, this book will be your ideal companion. With the inclusion of many recipes for both cures and brines, it will have you producing prize hams and rollmop herrings in no time. ISBN 978-1-904871-23-1

The Cheese Making Book
By Paul Peacock

Whether you plan to run your own dairy or to simply produce occasional brie for your own table, this book contains all the information you will need to guide you through the early tenetative steps. It also includes many recipes and a resource section which will give you the confidence to take your cheese making to whatever level you wish, whether delighting your friends with a beautiful stilton, or walking away with your first rosette at the local show! ISBN 978-1-904871-24-8

Other titles published by
The Good Life Press Ltd

A Cut Above the Rest (DVD) butchering techniques for
livestock producers
A Polytunnel Companion by Jayne Neville
The Shepherd's Pup (DVD) with Derek Scrimgeour
An Introduction to Keeping Sheep by Jane Upton and Denis
Soden
How to Butcher Livestock and Game By Paul Peacock
Talking Sheepdogs by Derek Scrimgeour
The Cheese Making Book by Paul Peacock
The Sausage Book by Paul Peacock
The Secret Life of Cows by Rosamund Young
The Secret Life of the Farm (DVD) with Rosamund Young
The Smoking and Curing Book by Paul Peacock
Traditional Cattle Breeds and how to keep them by Peter King

The Good Life Press Ltd.
(Formerly Farming Books and Videos Ltd.)
PO Box 536
Preston
PR2 9ZY
Tel 01772 652693

www.thegoodlifepress.co.uk
www.farmingbooksandvideos.com

The Good Life Press Ltd also publishes
Home Farmer Magazine.

www.homefarmer.co.uk